"Robyn Henk is a passionate Chri... *trainer of women; an insightful, engaging teacher of the Word; a Christian who identifies with the broken and hurting in our world."*

KAY WARREN
Saddleback Church

"For anyone whose life is not what they dreamed it would be, B.L.E.S.S.E.D. *will reach into your heart and get it pumping again. Robyn Henk's message and insights enter new territory that only one who has dealt with her own shattered dreams could cover. Her unique principles for living will make a dreamer's heart soar."*

GARY SMALLEY
Author of *I Promise* and *The DNA of Relationships*

"What a great work on moving beyond your own limitations and into the astounding plans God has for your life."

STEPHEN ARTERBURN
Founder of New Life Ministries and author of *Every Woman's Battle*

"The only thing better than reading this fabulous work is to see and hear Robyn teach herself. She has taken the great and difficult experiences of her life and the lives of her extraordinary family and created an essential tool for us to benefit from. Thousands of lives have been inspired by her teachings for years. Finally we are blessed to hold her words in our hands. If you are one who strives to better yourself, you assuredly must read this book. Be ready, because this teaching is capable of changing your life forever."

TERRI GREEN
Author of *Simple Acts of Kindness* and cofounder of Simple Acts Ministries, Inc.

"Robyn Henk's words will not only capture your mind but your heart as well, and will bring you to a greater understanding of God's love for you."

DOUG FIELDS
Pastor of life development at Saddleback Church and author of
If Life Is a Piece of Cake, Why Am I Still Hungry?

"After adopting four children internationally and playing a role in thousands of other adoptions through our nonprofit agency, I can say without reservation that B.L.E.S.S.E.D. is the cry of every family who experiences the spirit of adoption. Robyn Henk communicates the blessing of adopting those others tend to call 'special-needs' children and makes it clear that taking such children into our homes is a blessing and not a sacrificial or noble deed."

BRIAN LUWIS
CEO of America World Adoption Association and author of *Adopted by Design*

"The book in your hands is a pearl—its truths come from great depth and pressure to form something very precious. Robyn's story and journey are a rare combination of velvet and steel. Humanity and divinity meet to make a life worthy of giving away in these pages. Make no mistake, B.L.E.S.S.E.D. is a book about power, resolve, and convictions that transform. Don't be fooled. This book will challenge, uplift, encourage, and move you to expect God to move and bless your life."

KENNY LUCK
Author of *Risk* and *Every Man, God's Man*, president and founder of Every Man Ministries, and men's pastor at Saddleback Church

Blessed

discovering God's

bigger dream

for you

ROBYN HENK

Tyndale House Publishers, Inc., Carol Stream, Illinois

Visit Tyndale's exciting Web site at www.tyndale.com

TYNDALE and Tyndale's quill logo are registered trademarks of Tyndale House Publishers, Inc.

B.L.E.S.S.E.D.: Discovering God's Bigger Dream for You

Designed by Jessie McGrath

Library of Congress Cataloging-in-Publication Data

Henk, Robyn.
  B.L.E.S.S.E.D. : discovering God's bigger dream for you / Robyn Henk.
    p. cm.
  Includes bibliographical references (p.   ).
  ISBN-13: 978-1-4143-0943-9 (sc)
  ISBN-10: 1-4143-0943-0
  1. Christian life. 2. Henk, Robyn. I. Title. II. BLESSED.
  BV4501.3H45 2006
  248.4—dc22   2006017690

Printed in the United States of America

12   11   10   09   08   07   06
7   6   5   4   3   2   1

DEDICATION

This legacy is dedicated to my family, through whom God
has blessed me abundantly. To Michelle, Teddy,
and Savannah; Joshua and Meghan; Nori; Christopher;
Nicholas, Polly, and Gabriel; Suzanne and Andy;
and most especially to my darling, supportive soul mate, Greg,
without whom this never could have been written.

I would like to thank all the wonderful people who helped me make
this legacy a reality. To Joanne, who put the thought into my head,
and Richard, who brought it to reality; to Denise and Bob
in Bar Harbor, who provided me with the perfect writing apartment.
To Sue and Lorenzo at L'Arche Daybreak, who made my stay
at The Cedars possible; and to Josh, who coordinated all the
Toronto details. And most especially to my many prayer partners
who have faithfully prayed these words into existence!

Finally, I want to thank my agent, Bucky Rosenbaum, and the
incredible team at Tyndale House Publishers for making the experience
of publishing this book an illustration of its message. In my wildest
dreams I could not have imagined such amazing blessings.
Every step has been a gift from God.

TABLE OF CONTENTS

Introduction

God has a dream for our lives! He desires to give us good things, and He wants us to live with purpose and significance. The experiences of my life have taught me that God's plans are bigger and better than anything we could ever imagine for ourselves, and that we can encounter His blessings no matter what circumstances we may be facing. God has a better plan, but before we can live God's dream for our lives, we must be willing to do what it takes to let go of our plans and learn how to live *blessed* lives. Lives in which we genuinely:

Believe in God's goodness, regardless of our circumstances.

Let go of our agendas and allow God to plan better lives for us.

Embrace reality by accepting the truth of our lives and letting God use them for His glory.

See from God's heart by training ourselves to view life from the Kingdom perspective.

Stay where we are while holding on to our faith and dependence on His providence.

Expect to be blessed, looking for and receiving God's fulfillment on a daily basis.

Dedicate it all to Christ. Live for the One who died for us!

It's important to realize that although God's love for all His creation is unconditional, His *blessings* are conditional. They depend on obedience to His commands and His will, on faithfulness to His

Word and His promises, and most of all, on our acceptance of His plan of salvation through Jesus Christ. Do you know that the Bible says, "There is salvation in no one else! God has given no other name under heaven by which we must be saved"?[1] If you are not sure what this means, read on!

God created us because He loves us and wants to have a relationship with us. But He is a holy God, and the sinful nature of humans has caused a break in that relationship. The Bible tells us that we all have fallen short of the glory that God intended for us when He created human beings.[2] But because of His love for us, God sent His Son, Jesus, to die for us, to suffer the price for our sin, and to restore us to our rightful relationship with God. On the cross, Jesus Christ took the consequences for sin so that we could be reconciled with Him. After Jesus died, He was buried, and on the third day after His death He rose again—having conquered death, the ultimate consequence of sin. He returned to heaven and promised that He would return again, one last time at the end of all things, to claim His rightful place as Lord of all lords, over all creation. Those who have accepted His free gift of restored relationship with God will live forever with Him throughout eternity.

Before you can receive Christ's sacrifice on your behalf and be restored once and for all in your relationship with God, you need to admit that you are not perfect. You are a sinner—someone who has fallen short of God's perfect standard—and you cannot restore your relationship with God on your own. In other words, you realize that you need Christ's sacrifice in order to be forgiven. Then you need to acknowledge that Jesus Christ is the eternal Son of God, who paid the price for your sin. Accept the incredible gift of forgiveness that He has bought on your behalf by His sacrificial death on the cross, and thank Him for giving you eternal life in heaven. Finally, you need to commit to living your life under His directorship by reading the Bible, following what it says, and joining in the fellowship of other believers. Once you have committed to that, you are ready to begin the wonderful journey of discovering God's dream for you.

In the following pages, I make many assertions about God's promises and His faithfulness to His Word. It is my hope to share with you how God has blessed my life and to give some insight into how you can share in the incredible blessings that God wants to pour into the lives of all His children. We hear countless messages these days— many that sound appealing, and some that sound true. God has given us a standard for how to test the messages we hear: His holy Word. In these pages I have endeavored to write the truth about my life and my relationship with God. However, as you read these words, I urge you to check them out for yourself. In the Bible, the apostle Paul said, "The Bereans were of more noble character than the Thessalonians, for they received the message with great eagerness and examined the Scriptures every day to see if what Paul said was true."[3] As you read this book, I encourage you to think carefully about the Scriptures I use and to trust God's Holy Spirit to make them clear to you.

It is my prayer that God will be glorified in my life and through my life experiences. May these words bring you blessing and perhaps a new perspective. Whether you've been a Christian for years or are just beginning to learn about faith, God has an amazing dream for your life. You have an opportunity to live "blessed" and be a part of His awesome design and purposes. He is just waiting for you to come to Him and claim it!

Believe in God's Goodness

THE BEGINNING

The LORD is just! He is my rock! There is no evil in him!
PSALM 92:15

THE BEGINNING

Accepting the true condition of our lives is one of the hardest and most important things we can ever accomplish. We grow up with dreams of what our lives should look like, based on our perceptions of where we've come from and our expectations of where we want to end up. Our plans come as much from our past as from our hopes of the future.

My dream was simple: motherhood. It's all I ever wanted. The sum of all my plans, ambitions, hopes, and desires was to have babies. Many babies. Some of my earliest memories include wanting my mother to give me a baby sister for my own. I was seven when my younger sister, Michelle, the fifth of the five children in my family, was born.

My older siblings were nine, ten, and eleven years older than I, and I truly was a loved and desired child. A devastating brain-stem injury at age one and polio at age five had made me the center of family attention and favor. The gentle care I received from every member of my family nurtured me back to full health, but the age difference between my siblings and me also made me a solitary child, which is probably why I so desired a "baby of my own" to take care of. Lo and behold, baby sister Michelle came along. Although my mothering skills were mainly practiced on a baby doll that my mother gave me to tend while she cared for my sister, I was smitten with nurturing. Before I went to school, my doll was bathed, fed, diapered, and laid down for a nap, where she would be safely swaddled until I rushed home in the afternoon to care for her. As my sister grew into a toddler and then a preschooler, my parents bought me a walking doll that I dressed in Michelle's hand-me-downs and "raised" to school age.

For as long as I can remember, my one and only dream was to be a mother.

Through junior high, high school, and college, I never had the dreams of my classmates to accomplish big things—to cure cancer or bring world peace. Eventually the counterculture of the late sixties and early seventies enveloped me and "liberated" my thinking. My dream was still to be a mother, but I was freed from the necessity of finding a husband. The hippie lifestyle had made my quest easier, so imagine my surprise when at twenty years old I found myself falling deeply in love with a civil engineer!

In September 1971, Greg and I were both working for the Colorado Highway Department when we met at an office picnic. It really was love at first sight—and what a sight we must have been: wing tip, suit-wearing Greg with barefoot, granny-skirted me! Our courtship was fast and wonderful; we were engaged by December and married by the following August.

Greg was five years older than I, from a family of five children himself, and his immediate goal was marriage and a family. Complete opposites in every way but our foundational belief in Jesus as Lord and a desire for children, we immediately settled down to start our own family. After almost two years of frustration, fertility tests, and treatments, all we had produced was month following month of heartbreak. The prognosis was inescapable. Due to a combination of factors, Greg and I would never produce children together.

I had been raised on my mother's adage, "Whenever God closes a door, somewhere He opens a window." Maybe adoption was our "window"!

We contacted our local adoption agency with high hopes, only to be told that they weren't accepting any new applications and we should call back in six months.

Six months later we didn't just call back. Instead, we thought a personal visit to social services might be more fruitful. Were we in for a surprise! We were immediately told that because of our young ages (I was twenty-three, Greg twenty-eight), we could only qualify for a healthy, white newborn—and the waiting list was more than eight years long! Age, race, and even physical problems didn't bother us. We just wanted to be parents—*now*. Nonetheless, those issues bothered the Colorado social services department—at least when it came to us.

"So you're telling us that we *only* qualify for a newborn now, but the wait is more than eight years long. By the time we're at the top of the list, we will be old enough to qualify for an older or special-needs child, which is what we want *now*."

"Exactly!"

"Are there 'special needs' children available now?"

"Oh, of course. We have quite a long list of older, mixed race, or special-needs children waiting for placement."

"So we are on a waiting list, and they are on a waiting list, but we don't qualify for each other?"

"Exactly!"

Ah, bureaucracy. You just gotta love it!

We went home depressed and dejected. Well, actually, *I* went home depressed and dejected. My husband is an engineer. In his mind, the "formula" for us added up to children; if this combination of factors didn't work, we'd find another. The pattern of our relationship was being defined in those months. If Greg sees the glass half full, I see the glass cracked and leaking and making a mess all over the place. I immediately begin the "what if" game and jump to the worst possible scenarios on how the situation will end; Greg gets strategic and asks what our next step is. I get depressed and withdrawn; Greg gets energized and takes action. Although it seems that God has a sense of humor when it comes to relationships, our differences are exactly what balance us and make us "better together." My tendency to process an issue to its extreme moderates Greg's tendency to act too quickly; likewise, his energy motivates my despondency.

Yet it was to be my bout of "blues" that offered us the next step. Sitting at home alone, with the drapes drawn and feeling *very* sorry for my pitiful, childless plight, with no ambition to do anything but watch TV, I turned on the noon news. Either it was a slow news day or God was the station manager that day, because the lead story was about a group of children who were arriving at Denver's Stapleton Airport from Vietnam. Waiting at the concourse were their excited adoptive parents. The reporter pushed her microphone into the face of one of the anxious mothers and asked, "How are you feeling?" (They must teach that question in Reporting 101.)

"Oh," the mother gushed, "we've waited SOOO long for this day!"

"How long have you been waiting?"

"Six months!"

"Six months? Six months! You can't even make a baby in six months!" I shouted at the television.

The adoption agency's name was FCVN, Friends of Children of Vietnam. It was March 1, 1975. For decades Vietnam had been a country divided: North Vietnam under the primarily Communist dictatorship of Ho Chi Minh, and South Vietnam under Western-allied government. In 1961 as the political struggle escalated into civil war, President Kennedy sent four hundred American troops to assist the South Vietnamese government. American involvement grew steadily for the next fourteen years, and although it was never officially declared a war, it was the longest military conflict in American history, claiming over fifty-five thousand American lives. Greg called FCVN the morning of March 2, 1975, and they laid out the process for us. Step one: Get the forms to start our dossier. Step two: Contact a social services agency for a home study. FCVN worked closely with Catholic Social Services, so we gave them a call. That would be the last easy step of the process! The rest became a whirlwind of documents, affidavits, doctor's appointments (Why do we need blood tests for syphilis? We're *adopting*!), all happening against the headlines of Vietnam's imminent demise.

We had contacted Catholic Social Services and received a verbal agreement that they would conduct our home study for FCVN and get back to us to set a date. Every few days we called FCVN to check on our file. *Did we remember to include three copies of our marriage certificate? Did we remember four copies of last year's tax forms? Did our references come in?* We used any reason as an excuse for them to dig out our file and put it on top of the stacks of files that the agency was feverishly trying to process before the impending and inevitable fall of Vietnam's capital city of Saigon. The staff was working overtime to get as many orphans placed as they could while it was still possible. Meanwhile, Greg and I continued to work on the stacks of forms, writing our "history" and filling out forms for a foreign government that wouldn't be in power long enough to read them.

March flew into April. Then, on April 4, 1975, our world ended. A C5 transport jet, filled with Vietnamese orphans en route to American homes, crashed and burned on takeoff, killing 155 children and care workers. Our world faded into black. American personnel were frantically pulling out of the country, and these were among the last children that could be rescued from Vietnam. Any possibility of our adopting a child from Vietnam was ended. There would be no more flights, no more children coming to America. My dream of motherhood crashed in the rice paddy that day.

Our bodies had conspired against us—we couldn't produce children.

Our county had conspired against us—we couldn't adopt local children.

And now world events had conspired against us—our last hope was gone.

I was about to learn the greatest lesson of my life, which would also become the message of my life: *God is good, and His plan is best!* But before I could accept God's plan for my life, I had to want His plan. And before I could want it, I had to believe that His way was better than my way.

We live in an independent culture. We prize our ability to "do for ourselves," and we are proud of our own accomplishments. But the only way we can receive God's plan for our lives is when we become *convinced* that His way is better. That means we must absolutely believe that God truly is good, that He wants only good things for us, and that He will give only good things to us.

BELIEVING IN GOD'S GOODNESS

Life and circumstances combine to shape our perception of what is good and what is not. Culture attempts to define our idea of goodness, but Jesus attributed the title to God alone. "Why do you call me good?" Jesus asked. "Only God is truly good."[1]

If we desire to live truly blessed lives, to discover God's dreams and purposes, we must choose to believe in the unchanging goodness of God and the unquestionable goodness of everything He does and provides. Goodness is His unalterable nature, the definition of His character, and the quality of His being. He is the Good Shepherd, the source of every good and worthy thing, and the constructor and completer of His good works. But how does God define the word *good?* If we are going to believe intentionally in God's goodness, we need to have a foundational concept of what *good* means. Otherwise we may buy into the world's definition or our own self-centered ideas and discover that God isn't remotely like those things. For instance, if *good* means comfortable, easy, or trouble free, then we will sooner or later discover that everything God gives us in this life doesn't live up to those definitions. Likewise, if we don't have a firm idea of what God considers good, then the first hard thing that happens to us can cause us to fear God and reject or resent His plan. If we are going to genuinely believe that God is good, we must begin by finding out what *good* means.

THE GOODNESS OF WHO GOD IS

Goodness is an attribute of God; the Bible tells us that it is part of His very nature and the standard of everything He does. The psalms are the "songbook" of the Bible, the poems and anthems written to be read or sung aloud in worship, praise, and confession to God, proclaiming His nature and character. Psalm 23, perhaps the best known of all the psalms, provides a key to God's character by describing Him as our Good Shepherd.

> The LORD is my shepherd; I have all that I need. He lets
> me rest in green meadows; he leads me beside peaceful
> streams. He renews my strength. He guides me along
> right paths, bringing honor to his name.

The opening lines of this psalm show us God's intended role as the Shepherd of His people. A shepherd is a guide, a protector, a provider. He supplies everything His flock needs. He brings them to places of refreshment when they are weary—*green meadows* of provision and nourishment, places where comfort and sustenance are provided for their souls. God tells us that He has given us His Word, the Holy Bible, to feed our souls: "People do not live by bread alone; rather, we live by every word that comes from the mouth of the LORD."[2]

The shepherd renews his flock's strength when they are weak. He provides times of peace and calm so they can regain their strength and rest. Scripture tells us that God created the seventh day to be set aside just for rest! What a gift from our Shepherd. Most of us don't acknowledge this gift anymore, and more is the pity. In this stressed-out, over-committed world, we lose 1,248 hours of God-given time to rest every year. The Lord Himself once asked Moses, "How long will these people refuse to obey my commands and instructions? They must realize that the Sabbath is the LORD's gift to you."[3]

The shepherd is also a guide; he leads his sheep along the right and safe pathways. When we follow His Word, God leads us along right paths—ways of integrity, moral correctness, and justice. Psalm 119 tells us that our happiness is found "along the path of [God's] commands" and that God's Word is "a lamp to guide my feet and a light for my path."[4] The prophet Isaiah assured that "for those who are righteous, the way is not steep and rough. You are a God who does what is right, and you smooth out the path ahead of them."[5] When we choose to believe in God's goodness, we choose a Shepherd who protects us, provides for us, and directs us.

Psalm 23 continues:

> Even when I walk through the darkest valley, I will not
> be afraid, for you are close beside me. Your rod and your
> staff protect and comfort me.

God does not remove us from the reality of our world or the difficulties of life, but as our Good Shepherd, He never leaves us to face them alone. He is beside us, using His rod to defend us and His staff to draw us close. He tells us that when we pass through the fires and storms of our lives,[6] He will be with us; we will not face our disasters and heartaches alone if we choose to follow Him through our valleys. And in the ultimate battle, the battle for eternity, the Good Shepherd lays down His life for His flock. Jesus said:

> I am the good shepherd. The good shepherd sacrifices his life for the sheep. A hired hand will run when he sees a wolf coming. He will abandon the sheep because they don't belong to him and he isn't their shepherd. And so the wolf attacks them and scatters the flock. The hired hand runs away because he's working only for the money and doesn't really care about the sheep. I am the good shepherd; I know my own sheep, and they know me, just as my Father knows me and I know the Father. So I sacrifice my life for the sheep. I have other sheep, too, that are not in this sheepfold. I must bring them also. They will listen to my voice, and there will be one flock with one shepherd.[7]

Christ as our Good Shepherd gave His life for us so that we could always be part of God's flock—and thereby always be the recipients of His goodness. He isn't like any other shepherd or leader; He will never desert in the face of danger. He knows us. He knows our lives—what we are going through, what we need, what we yearn for and dream about. And He will not rest until *all* His sheep are accounted for.

But the goodness of God goes beyond His shepherding us. A shepherd is indeed a provider, protector, guide, and leader, but the shepherd does not have a personal relationship with his sheep. Psalm 23 changes the analogy now, and we see our Lord as our *host*.

> You prepare a feast for me in the presence of my enemies. You honor me by anointing my head with oil. My cup overflows with blessings.

God's provision goes beyond our necessities. His graciousness overflows on our behalf. He sets more than a dinner place for us; He prepares a feast in our honor! In Isaiah, God reassures His children, "Do not be afraid . . . my chosen one. For I will pour out abundant water to quench your thirst and to irrigate your parched fields. And I will pour out my Spirit on your descendants, and my blessings on your children. They will thrive like watered grass, like willows on a riverbank."[8] And in Malachi, He declares, "I will open the windows of heaven for you. I will pour out a blessing so great you won't have enough room to take it in! Try it! Put me to the test!"[9] God promises to pour out His abundant blessings upon us in this life, and even more in the next. Jesus tells us that He Himself has prepared a place for us in heaven, and that the Kingdom of Heaven is like a wedding feast waiting for the guests to arrive.[10]

Psalm 23 ends by assuring us of God's goodness (that word again!), which pursues us, along with His unfailing love. We don't have to run after God's goodness. He chases after us with it! He *wants* to pour out His good things on us. And He will not withdraw that goodness from us—it's forever!

> Surely your goodness and unfailing love will pursue me
> all the days of my life, and I will live in the house of the
> LORD forever.

God's goodness is the source of all He gives us and does for us. The more we understand what He considers good, the more we can trust that He *is* as good as He says He is!

THE GOODNESS OF WHAT GOD GIVES

It is God's nature to give. Everything He gives is good, and all that He gives flows from His goodness. Regardless of our circumstances and whether or not it seems that God is listening to our prayers, God is giving His children good things. The apostle Matthew writes that Jesus taught:

> You parents—if your children ask for a loaf of bread, do
> you give them a stone instead? Or if they ask for a fish,
> do you give them a snake? Of course not! So if you sinful
> people know how to give good gifts to your children,
> how much more will your heavenly Father give good
> gifts to those who ask him.[11]

God's concept of goodness goes far beyond our comprehension or expectations, and often beyond our notice. When we look for the "good" things that the world promotes (prestige, popularity, prosperity), we end up missing the better things—the *best things*—God is offering: His presence, His provision, His power, and His plan for our lives. Jesus said:

> Look at the lilies and how they grow. They don't work
> or make their clothing, yet Solomon in all his glory was
> not dressed as beautifully as they are. And if God cares
> so wonderfully for flowers that are here today and
> thrown into the fire tomorrow, he will certainly care for
> you. Why do you have so little faith? And don't be con-
> cerned about what to eat and what to drink. Don't worry
> about such things. These things dominate the thoughts
> of unbelievers all over the world, but your Father already
> knows your needs. Seek the Kingdom of God above all
> else, and he will give you everything you need. So don't
> be afraid, little flock. For it gives your Father great hap-
> piness to give you the Kingdom.[12]

What is the Kingdom? It's the things that God desires: caring for the disenfranchised, the poor, and the needy; visiting those who are in prison and alone; giving aid to the sick and dying; loving others enough to share the Good News of Christ with them; forgiving those who have hurt us; and putting the needs of others before our own. It gives God pleasure to provide for His children, but when we focus on the things of this world instead of concentrating on the Kingdom of God, we miss so much of what God is doing in our lives. We miss the power He gives us to endure through our hard times, we miss the provision God gives us to share with others, and we miss the inner confidence God gives us, the peace that can calm our troubled souls even in the midst of a troubled world.

James wrote:

> Whatever is good and perfect comes down to us from
> God our Father, who created all the lights in the heav-
> ens. He never changes or casts a shifting shadow. He
> chose to give birth to us by giving us his true word. And
> we, out of all creation, became his prized possession.[13]

We can count on the consistency of God's goodness. He will never change His definition or disguise His good things to look like something they are not. Our culture changes its definition of *good* every new fashion season. The world makes sin look good; it makes evil look beneficial; it makes selfishness and self-centeredness look healthy and normal. The world lies. Only the things that come from God are and remain *truly* good: His standards, His commands, His will, His plan for us, His chosen and precious children.

God gives us the right to be called His own children: "To all who believed him and accepted him, he gave the right to become children of God."[14] He gives us His own Spirit of life as a seal of His promises to us: "We know how dearly God loves us, because he has given us the Holy Spirit to fill our hearts with his love."[15] The Spirit resides in us and gives us spiritual gifts that allow us to grow in our faith and encourage others in theirs. "There are different kinds of spiritual gifts, but the same Spirit is the source of them all."[16]

But the most wonderful good gift of all is the gift of eternal life in Christ. The Bible tells us that in the end, the only thing the world will leave us is the finality of death, but God has given us the ultimate gift. The world gives us only what we have earned, but God gives us the free gift of life everlasting in Christ![17]

These are God's definitions of *good things*! To believe in the goodness of God means believing that everything from Him is good, regardless of how it feels to us at the moment. It means we can resist the world's temptations because we know He has something better. It even means we can face the consequences of our wrong choices with courage and conviction because He will give us the power and guidance to persevere. It means we can withstand the difficult circumstances that come from living in an imperfect and deteriorating world because we know that He will sustain us and provide for us during our hard times. And though not everything we experience in this life may be good, it means we can trust that God desires to give us the things that will ultimately empower us to live lives that give testimony to His goodness. For how would it glorify God to give His children anything but the best?

THE GOODNESS OF WHAT GOD DOES

In the beginning God created the heavens and the earth. The earth was formless and empty, and darkness covered the deep waters. And the Spirit of God was hovering over the surface of the waters. Then God said, "Let there be light," and there was light. And God saw that the light was good. Then he separated the light from the darkness. . . . So God created human beings in his own image. In the image of God he created them; male and female he created them. Then God blessed them and said,

"Be fruitful and multiply. Fill the earth and govern it.
Reign over the fish in the sea, the birds in the sky,
and all the animals that scurry along the ground." Then
God said, "Look! I have given you every seed-bearing
plant throughout the earth and all the fruit trees for your
food. And I have given every green plant as food for all
the wild animals, the birds in the sky, and the small
animals that scurry along the ground—everything
that has life." And that is what happened. Then God
looked over all he had made, and he saw that it was very
good![18]

The opening words of the Bible begin with a description of what
God considers good. He created humans in His own pattern so that
we could have a relationship with Him. He also created every form of
sustenance and provision that His creation would need to survive.
Everything that flows from God is good. From His creation to His
plan of redemption to the eventual total reconciliation of His creation
to Himself, everything God does represents His goodness. Although
it was humans who broke relationship with God, it was God who
planned and provided the means of reconciliation.

God showed his great love for us by sending Christ to
die for us while we were still sinners. And since we have
been made right in God's sight by the blood of Christ,
he will certainly save us from God's condemnation. For
since our friendship with God was restored by the death
of his Son while we were still his enemies, we will certainly be saved through the life of his Son. So now we
can rejoice in our wonderful new relationship with God
because our Lord Jesus Christ has made us friends of
God.[19]

By God's goodness we were restored to a relationship with Him in this lifetime and spared from His judgment in the next! The goodness of God the Father provided the way for this relationship, and the goodness of God the Son achieved it: "The Son of Man came not to be served but to serve others and to give his life as a ransom for many."[20] The goodness of God the Spirit allows us to be transformed by it. "The Holy Spirit produces this kind of fruit in our lives: love, joy, peace, patience, kindness, goodness, faithfulness, gentleness, and self-control. There is no law against these things!"[21]

Restoration, reconciliation, transformation: the goodness of what God does! How does God define *good?* By who He is, by what He gives, and by what He does. "The LORD is just! He is my rock! There is no evil in him!"[22]

TRUST

When we genuinely believe in God's goodness, we begin to trust Him. We desire His will for our lives because we realize that His will is better than anything we could want for ourselves. We want to do things His way because we trust that His way is best, that His way will bring deeper joy and significance to our lives. We trust that what He has told us is good and that He will bring good into our lives and the lives of those we love.

> Taste and see that the LORD is good. Oh, the joys of
> those who take refuge in him! Fear the LORD, you his
> godly people, for those who fear him will have all they
> need. Even strong young lions sometimes go hungry, but
> those who trust in the LORD will lack no good thing.[23]

When we know deep in our hearts that we can rely on God to provide the good things we need, when we need them, we are able to live our lives with courage, confidence, and conviction!

COURAGE

> The LORD is good, a strong refuge when trouble comes.
> He is close to those who trust in him.[24]

When we trust in the goodness of God, we are free to live with greater courage. Our fears fade. Our worries about the future begin to dissipate when we realize that our future is in the hands of a good and almighty God. Our fear of rejection begins to diminish when we recognize that we are accepted by a good and loving Father. Our dread of the unknown begins to decrease when we appreciate that we are in the care of our good Protector. Our anxieties of inadequacy are dispelled as we understand that we have access to all the resources of a good and caring Provider.

CONFIDENCE

> Do not throw away this confident trust in the Lord.
> Remember the great reward it brings you![25]

When we trust in the goodness of God, we are free to live with greater confidence. We can trust His direction for our lives because we can count on Him to give us truthful insight, superior wisdom, and beneficial counsel for the choices we have to make on a daily basis. Proverbs 3:5-6 tells us that we can trust in the Lord with all our heart and that we don't have to depend on our own limited understanding. If we seek His will in all the things we do, He will direct the paths of our lives. When we believe in the goodness of God, we can trust that He will lead us *only* into good things!

CONVICTION

When we trust in the goodness of God, we are free to live with deeper conviction and purpose. Trusting in God's goodness means believing in His constancy, regardless of how momentary events appear. It means we can have the confidence to hold to godly principles and priorities, regardless of their popularity, current cultural "correctness," or what others may think or say. It means having a constant moral compass that we can be completely sure of. It means living a life of significance because we are living with godly purpose. Isaiah 26:4 assures us that we can trust in the Lord always, because He is the *eternal Rock!*

Scripture not only affirms His goodness but also assures us that He has planned out good lives for us and that He wants good things for us. When we look closely at the Word of God and His definition of what is good, and when we pay close attention to what He is doing in our lives, we will begin to see and trust in the good things He is doing.

QUESTIONS

The author mentions the despair she felt after all the paths to starting a family seemingly closed. God appeared distant and uncaring. Have you ever felt this way? What circumstances prompted it? How did you deal with it?

What are some of the fears that you struggle with? How would it help you to know that a good God cares about your fears?

What difficult decisions are you facing right now? How would knowing that God's ways always result in good, help you in the decisions you have to make?

Consider the moral and ethical climate of the world today. How does trusting that God's standards are consistent with His goodness change or affect your perception of what is happening in our societies and families?

What beliefs or practices (habits, lifestyle, and attitudes) do you need to address in order to trust God's goodness in your own life?

2

Let Go of Your Agenda

GETTING ON TRACK

> I will open the windows of heaven for you. I will pour out a blessing
> so great you won't have enough room to take it in!
> MALACHI 3:10

A NEW WAY

When the C5 plane crashed that April morning on the outskirts of Saigon, I felt that all my hopes and dreams and plans—in fact, my whole future—had crashed with it. My mother had always told me, "Whenever God closes a door, somewhere He opens a window." She never told me what happens when the window shatters.

Even now, twenty-eight years later, I can conjure up the pain, darkness, and sense of utter loneliness that I felt in my despair. Greg and I had both come from fertile, baby-loving families. I can remember thinking as a young girl, *I just couldn't live if I couldn't have children.* I was discovering that a broken heart doesn't kill you—it just feels like it.

Two days after the crash, more on autopilot than anything else, I went down to the offices of FCVN to turn in the last of our documents.

Of course there was no reason to now, but it gave me something to do and a reason to leave the house. Greg, the eternal optimist, insisted, "It couldn't hurt. At least our file will be complete." (Just like an engineer. No matter what, finish the project!)

The office had always been like the center of a beehive, literally buzzing with activity, ringing telephones, and flying papers. This day it was still busy, but with a heaviness of grief. Many of the workers' friends had died on that plane, as well as the children who had been placed for adoption. I dropped off the papers and turned to leave. In the hallway, as I approached the steps, a woman was sitting at a school desk, addressing envelopes. She asked who I was and why I was there. I explained that I was turning in the last of our forms, though of course there was no hope now. She smiled and said that there was always hope! Did I know that Lutheran Social Services was starting a pilot adoption program in Manila, Philippines? They were just now taking applications and hoped to place their first few children in the near future. She scribbled down a name and phone number and told me to give them a call. To this day, even though I became very close with the staff of FCVN and volunteered often in their office, I have no idea who that woman was. I never saw her again.

Greg called the number immediately. We began to fill out more forms and felt a glimmer of new hope.

On March 30, Da Nang, the second-largest city of Vietnam, had been captured by the North Vietnamese, and Saigon was attacked on all three sides. American and South Vietnamese government officials and citizens alike were fleeing the country—but an estimated seventy thousand orphans remained behind. On April 3, President Gerald Ford announced the plans for Operation Babylift. Thirty flights were planned to evacuate as many of the babies and young children as possible. More than two thousand children were flown out and adopted by American families. Most of these children had already been officially placed for adoption in the United States months before the fall of Saigon, and their families had been waiting for their arrival. But now because of their hasty evacuation they needed temporary facilities until they were "processed" and united with their families. Because two of the largest placement agencies were located in the Denver area, it became one of the central locations of care for the children. Care centers were set up and volunteers worked around the clock to care for the hungry, confused, and sometimes sick children who had arrived from halfway around the world.

Yet no one could have prepared me for the events of May 15, 1975. It had been six weeks since that fateful plane crash. Though the calendar doesn't lie, in my memory it was one of the longest passages of time in my life. Sometimes I think it is possible for time to stand still, or at least to move much slower than the standard seconds and minutes. Each moment lived in sorrow is lengthened almost beyond endurance. Though utter despair had given way to a slight glimmer of hope, I had no idea that God was just about to open the floodgates of blessing. Around two o'clock that Thursday afternoon, the telephone rang. It was our caseworker at Catholic Social Services. We were being considered for a baby girl who had arrived on the airlift. She had a cleft lip and cleft palate. "Think about it, and meet me at my office tomorrow morning at ten o'clock."

First call: Greg!

Second call: a pediatrician. What in the world are *cleft lip* and *cleft palate?*

The doctor explained that cleft lip and/or palate is one of the most common birth defects; about one in eight hundred babies is born with some form of it. Basically, clefting occurs when the right and left sides of the upper lip and/or roof of the mouth don't fuse together properly during the early stages of pregnancy, leaving a gap—or "cleft." Several surgeries are usually involved to close the gaps, and some speech therapy and orthodontia may be required as the child grows up, depending how severely the teeth, gums, and lips are affected.

Okay, that didn't sound like anything dreadful; certainly we could deal with it. More important, what did "You're being *considered*" mean? Were others being considered for this baby as well? Was it like some competition—the parents with the best answers win?

It seems pretty silly now to look back on how much angst one ill-chosen word could cause, but that night certainly produced as much prayer and soul-searching and preparation as any all-nighter before a final exam. The next morning Greg and I were down at the office bright and early. Finally we were ushered into the cluttered office of our social worker. We were solemnly advised that the placement process could take a couple of days, but we had the option of seeing the baby before we made up our minds. There was no question for us. Of course we wanted her, but we'd also love to see her as soon as possible. We were asked to step out of the office and help ourselves to a cup of coffee in the foyer (it's amazing what people call coffee) while the social worker made arrangements for us to visit her at the care center.

Twenty minutes later, he announced, "You can go pick her up in half an hour if you want!"

What? She's ours? Now? I placed an excited phone call to my neighbor Carol. "Guess what? I'm bringing home a baby! Can you believe it?" Then a call to my mom, then to each of my sisters. The last call was to the pediatrician whom I had talked to the day before. How quickly could we schedule an appointment?

No one but our references had known that we were pursuing Vietnamese adoption. The process had been so frustrating and emotional, we couldn't bear being asked more questions by family or friends. Over the last few years we had endured so many already:

"When are you guys going to settle down and have kids?"

"Aren't you pregnant yet?"

"What do you hear from the county? Are you *still* on the waiting list?"

"Wow, you'll be old enough to be grandparents by the time you get a baby!"

Though people meant well, each question and quip ripped at our hearts. Needless to say, our announcement came as quite a surprise!

The next thing we knew, we were holding in our arms the most precious, tiny baby girl we had ever seen. Three months old, and barely five pounds, she was the most beautiful little thing I had ever laid eyes on. It wasn't until we got to the car that we realized that we didn't own one thing for babies. Not even a diaper!

When we got home, waiting on our front porch was every baby item we would need for months: diapers, clothing, a changing table, a cradle. Carol had rallied all the neighbors on our behalf—or really, on our daughter's behalf. Moments later my sisters arrived, and I realized that not only did I have no idea *what* to feed our baby, I had even less of an idea *how* to feed a child with cleft lip and palate. My sister Nancy, who had been a registered nurse, went with me to the appointment with our pediatrician that afternoon. After a complete physical exam, the doctor pronounced our baby dehydrated and undernourished but reasonably healthy. He recommended a soy formula, and because she wasn't able to suck, he showed me how to feed her by pinching a spout on a small paper cup, then slowly dripping the formula into her mouth. Because the cleft palate leaves an opening into the inner-ear area, babies are susceptible to ear infections, so we needed to feed her slowly, in an upright position to keep the milk flowing in the right direction to her tummy. Then the doctor sent me on my way. By evening, with the help of my sisters, I was actually starting to believe that I was indeed a mom. We put the baby's cradle next to our bed, and I slept with my hand on her all night—just to make sure she was *really* ours.

We decided to name her Michelle and keep her original name, Thi Loan, for her middle name. Michelle means "loved by God," and Loan means "phoenix," the mythical bird that rises from its own ashes. It seemed impossible that it had been only weeks since I'd seen the news report about babies coming to the United States from Vietnam. From the ashes of war and despair, God had brought us this precious blessing!

When God shuts a door, somewhere He opens a window. When God shatters the window, He pours down His blessings through the broken panes—if we can keep from boarding up before the storm hits. "We know that God causes everything to work together for the good of those who love God and are called according to his purpose for them."[1]

The greatest blessing of our lives had just poured in through the shattered window of frustration, infertility, and despair. But before this blessing could come to us, we had to first completely let go of our agenda. We had to accept that our way wasn't going to work. We had to open our hearts and minds to new possibilities. Giving up our dreams, our plans, and our way requires surrendering a prideful sense of our own significance. We must realize our powerlessness to be truly effective in achieving our deepest desires and needs. It is an emptying of self, but to be empty is to be ready for filling!

LETTING GO OF YOUR AGENDA

Whether or not we are intentional about it, we all have agendas for our lives and for our futures. Some of our agendas may be more immediate than others, some more "official" than others, some more sophisticated than others—but they exist. We are not simply drifting through life. The choices we make, the priorities we set, the standards we live by, and the plans and dreams we hope for are all a part of our personal designs. Few of us have actually taken the time to examine our life principles or formally establish the values on which we are intentionally building our lives, but even if we have not officially developed a life mission statement, our consistent pattern of decisions and actions illustrates the master plan by which we are living.

God has a better design for our lives than any we can devise for ourselves. He is our creator, our provider, and our sustainer. His agenda for His children is for a blessed life, a righteous life—a life lived for a greater purpose than we could ever establish for ourselves using the world's standards and practices. Because God has a greater perspective, one that includes all time and space and potential, His dreams for us are bigger than we could ever imagine. Because His vision includes all people and all events, His plans for us are more intricate and far reaching than we could contrive. Because His truth is absolute, His power is supreme, and His love is greater and deeper than any we could experience without Him, His ways are more dynamic than we could ever envision on our own.

To accept God's agenda, we must first be willing to set our own plans aside, and then wait for His plan to unfold in our lives. But it is not easy to let go of our own goals, our own dreams, and especially our own ways of doing things. After all, being "in control" is not only encouraged but also admired and rewarded in our society. We grow up learning that we need to stay in control of our emotions, our actions, and our possessions. For some of us, like Greg and me, circumstances will make it evident that we don't have the command over our lives that we thought we did. Whether we are forced by circumstances or motivated by good sense, if we want to live lives that are blessed beyond our wildest dreams, we must be willing to give up our agendas and accept the better plans that God our Father has designed for each of us.

ACCEPT GOD'S TRUTH

What we believe to be true affects every part of our lives. It establishes our belief systems, our moral codes, our ambitions, and our definitions of success and failure. It defines how we see ourselves in relation to others and even how we see our place in the progression of history. Our beliefs form the basis for what we value as significant and what consequences we anticipate for our actions. Before we can accept God's design for our lives, we must establish what will be the foundation of our lives: the social, ethical, and moral codes of God, or the social, ethical, and moral codes of the world. One is absolute; one is constantly changing. One is written; the other is ambiguous.

The Bible is the written Word of God. Not only has this been testified to and tested through the ages, it is proven by the lives of people who have lived according to it. The Bible states emphatically that "all Scripture is inspired by God and is useful to teach us what is true and to make us realize what is wrong in our lives. It corrects us when we are wrong and teaches us to do what is right. God uses it to prepare and equip his people to do every good work."[2]

Though God used men to write down His words, it was He, not they, who authored Scripture. Peter reminds us, "Above all, you must realize that no prophecy in Scripture ever came from the prophet's own understanding or from human initiative. No, these prophets were moved by the Holy Spirit, and they spoke from God."[3] The psalmist praised the truth and eternal nature of God's words: "The very essence of your words is truth; all your just regulations will stand forever."[4]

To begin to let go of our agendas and take the steps that open the pathway to God's plan for our lives, we need to decide, once and for all, if we believe that God's Word is true for *every* condition, circumstance, and situation. We need to ask whether we accept it as our standard for right and wrong, for true and false, for good and evil. We must assess whether we intend to do everything in our power to establish the Word of God as our foundation—the basis of every standard, principle, attitude, motive, and action. The more we build on this foundation, the more fully we can embrace the good things God has intended for us. We will trust Him more because we will understand His priorities, His will, and the way He works. We will step out in faith and risk trying life His way. And our faith will not disappoint us! God has a history of faithfulness. His Word attests to it: "Our ancestors trusted in you, and you rescued them. They cried out to you and were saved. They trusted in you and were never disgraced."[5]

The Bible is the record of God's promises to us and the history of how He has fulfilled, how He is fulfilling, and how He will fulfill those promises.

> God has given both his promise and his oath. These two
> things are unchangeable because it is impossible for God
> to lie. Therefore, we who have fled to him for refuge can
> have great confidence as we hold to the hope that lies
> before us. This hope is a strong and trustworthy anchor
> for our souls.[6]

ACCEPT YOUR POWERLESSNESS

One of the primary obstacles we have to "letting go and letting God" control our lives is our illusion that we somehow have the power to accomplish significant things on our own. Jesus reminded us that we can't even change one hair on our heads from black to white or add one extra day to our lives![7] In fact, Jesus said that anything we accomplish that is not rooted in Him and in God's plan will ultimately amount to nothing. "Yes, I am the vine; you are the branches. Those who remain in me, and I in them, will produce much fruit. For apart from me you can do nothing."[8]

Scripture tells us that there will come a time when everything we have ever done will be judged by its significance to the Kingdom of God.

> On the judgment day, fire will reveal what kind of work
> each builder has done. The fire will show if a person's
> work has any value. If the work survives, that builder will

receive a reward. But if the work is burned up, the builder
will suffer great loss. The builder will be saved, but like
someone barely escaping through a wall of flames.[9]

In this world we have the capacity to acquire possessions, power,
prestige, and even popularity. It is possible to feel significant, for a
while; it is possible to produce an impression of significance, for a time;
it is even possible to devise plans that will influence others, until a new
concept comes around. These acquisitions are fleeting. Time and circumstance will eventually erode these things, because they are based
on the temporary capabilities of the world. God created us to last forever and to live forever with Him in His Kingdom. Therefore, only
what is birthed and developed in and for the Kingdom will endure. For
each one of us, God has a Kingdom plan. It is our eternal legacy. But we
cannot achieve or even receive it in our own power. It is only when we
surrender our attempts to achieve our own agendas that God finally
begins to present His plan for our lives.

God told the prophet Isaiah, "I have a plan for the whole earth, a
hand of judgment upon all the nations. The Lord of Heaven's Armies
has spoken—who can change his plans? When his hand is raised, who
can stop him?"[10]

ACCEPT NEW POSSIBILITIES

God's design often seems beyond our comprehension. He does things
differently than we would; He sees potential where we see problems.
A crucial step to accepting new possibilities is to abandon the need to
understand. Quite honestly, we cannot understand God's ways!
Sometimes they make more sense to us than at other times, but the
fact is:

"My thoughts are nothing like your thoughts," says the
LORD. "And my ways are far beyond anything you could

imagine. For just as the heavens are higher than the
earth, so my ways are higher than your ways and my
thoughts higher than your thoughts."[11]

There comes a time when we must let go of our need to know.
Why did God intend that our daughter would come from halfway
around the world and be born in the midst of battle? Of all the children from Vietnam and all the families wanting them—why us? Why
were we the fortunate ones? We can't begin to understand why; all we
know is, she did, she was, and we are. God tells us that we are not
capable of understanding His thoughts and His ways—and thank
goodness we're not! Imagine a God who is no greater than our feeble
capacity to understand. Scary!

Once we let go of our need to figure it all out, we are finally in a
place where we can open our lives to greater possibilities. And when
we do that, there is no limit to what God will do—or how He will
choose to do it. The apostle Paul knew that. God chose him, a Phari-
see who had persecuted Christians, to be the one who brought His
message to the Gentiles. Paul wrote to the believers in the city of
Corinth:

> God chose things the world considers foolish in order to
> shame those who think they are wise. And he chose
> things that are powerless to shame those who are power-
> ful. God chose things despised by the world, things
> counted as nothing at all, and used them to bring to
> nothing what the world considers important. As a result,
> no one can ever boast in the presence of God.[12]

God likes to act in ways that will show His goodness—not our
abilities. I've come to realize that if we can do something completely
competently by our own abilities, in our own confidence and comfort

level, it probably isn't God's agenda for us. God's agenda goes beyond our capacity to achieve on our own.

The final step in letting go of our agendas is to irrevocably give back to God what is His—our lives. He has created, designed, and redeemed our lives, for us personally. When we give Him control, we are not guaranteed ease, comfort, or even necessarily pleasure, but we are guaranteed blessing. In the book of Malachi, God tells His people that if they are willing to let go of just 10 percent of what they own, He would "open the windows of heaven for you. I will pour out a blessing so great you won't have enough room to take it in!"[13] If God wants to greatly bless those who offer Him merely a portion of the things they own, how much more will He bless those who give Him their very lives? Over and over again in Scripture, God says that the ultimate offering He wants us to give Him is how we live our lives: in complete dependence on His ways.[14]

SURRENDER

The concept of surrender makes us uneasy. Bruce Springsteen sings, "No retreat, no surrender." The cultural idea of ultimate heroism is "Never surrender at any price!" and the epitome of total victory is the "unconditional surrender"[15] of the vanquished. Surrender denotes loss of control. When we are completely honest, we realize how out of control we really are when it comes to our security, our comfort, and even our safety. Recent world events graphically illustrate how vulnerable we are to attacks by people and nature. Our jobs are only as secure as the economy, and it seems that every week we hear about new threats to our health. Still, it can be frightening to hand the reins of our lives over to someone else . . . even if that someone is God. Maybe for some of us, *especially* if that someone is God. Sure, dramatic testimonies make for good listening (or reading), but how many of us want to live dramatic lives? We are afraid that if God gets control of us, the next thing we know we'll be missionaries in Africa! My friend

John recently received a relatively big investment payoff. Instead of celebrating, the poor man worried that now that he no longer had to work for a living, God would make him give up the job he loves and send him to some remote jungle to teach children (a nightmare for him!).

Surrender also denotes weakness and dependence. We all begin our lives in a state of weakness, and most of us will also end that way. The appeal of the helpless little baby who must depend upon those around her for safety, nourishment, health, and comfort becomes the heartache of the elderly, who increasingly find their independence slipping away. Because we dread depending on someone else, we hold tightly to the little control we believe we have. But if we are going to accept God's design for our lives, we must also allow Him to control how it plays out, and we must determine to live according to it. God has a better plan for every significant aspect of who we are, including our relationships, our abilities, and even our emotions. Surrendering our lives to God means letting Him direct every part.

RELATIONSHIPS

When we realize that the people God brings into our lives are part of His agenda for us, we begin to appreciate not only those people with whom we have developed relationships (such as our family, friends, coworkers, and neighbors) but also the significance of those "chance" encounters that surprise and sometimes annoy us. The most important of all of God's creation is people (we are the *only* part of creation that God created in His own image[16]), and thus the relationships we develop with God and each other have great value. Therefore, when we commit to living entirely dedicated to God's agenda, we begin to realize that there really is no such thing as happenstance. The people we cross paths with, run into, work next to, stand in line with, and sit next to on long cross-country flights may have been put in our paths by *intentional providence*. The Bible tells us to make the most out of every opportunity[17] and that we should treat strangers as if they were Jesus Himself. Sometimes the strangers we meet are actually messengers God has sent to us.[18]

This understanding opens our minds and hearts to the potential of the moment. Perhaps this person has something that God wants us to hear, see, learn, or feel. Maybe this person is someone outside of our immediate base of experience, someone with a different culture, viewpoint, or sensitivity, whom God has specifically placed in our path to soften our hearts, inform our minds, or expand our awareness. Or perhaps God wants to use us to speak to or touch this person's life in some unexpected and unrehearsed way. When we surrender *all* our plans to God's use (even that nap we intended to take on the plane), every person we meet becomes significant, because every person we meet is significant to God. A surrendered life is one that is aware, accepting, and open to the people God brings into it.

Surrendering our agendas enables us to let go of our attempts to control others and to realize that we can choose how much control we allow them to have over us. Because I had always been a people pleaser, I constantly found myself saying yes to people, commitments, and even phone solicitors that better sense told me to politely refuse. Then, when I was completely stressed out and overwhelmed, I would blame others for not doing *their* part! I was afraid that if I said no, people might think I was lazy or uncaring or not willing to do my part. I let what *I thought they thought about me* motivate my decisions. When I began to realize that God wants to direct what we obligate our time and energy to, it became easier for me to say no to others and to allow others to say no to me. When we don't feel controlled by others, we no longer need to control others. When we no longer feel used by others, we don't tend to use others. Instead, we begin to value and appreciate people.

God has a better plan for our relationships. He is not only the introducer of people into our lives, He is also the coordinator of our communities of influence and our acquaintances. That is not to say that we abandon all responsibility for our influence on our social community. In fact, when we submit our relationships to God, we realize more than ever our mutual dependence on the people He puts in our lives. We begin to appreciate that they are part of God's design for us and that we are a part of God's design for them! As a result, we find ourselves becoming more fully engaged with the people around us, through our conversations and observations. Knowing that each encounter is pregnant with "Kingdom potential," we really do care if the salesclerk is having a good day or not. We realize that we have the potential to impact each other's lives—even if only by making eye contact or leaving with a smile.

Recently I ran into a homeless couple panhandling on the streets. Usually I would cross the street or toss them some loose change, but that day I was struck by the thought that maybe this was an ordained encounter. Instead of looking away, I approached them and I saw them—I mean, I really saw them. Looking full into their eyes, I asked their names, I asked them to tell me their story—why they were on the streets, what brought them to this place. In the end, I gave them money to feast at the all-you-can-eat buffet down the street. I even walked there with them! Now to be honest, I don't know if they used the money for the buffet or walked down the street to the closest bar. I don't know if their story was true. I can't even be sure that their names were real . . . but it doesn't matter. In those moments, God brought us together. For a few moments, two people felt *seen* and that their lives meant something to someone, and I was free to care for them without requiring them to thank me, repay me, or even tell me the truth. I was free just to experience this moment God had orchestrated.

I can surrender my personal relationship needs to God as well. Thanks to Christ Jesus, I now can enjoy full, intimate, satisfying communion with the Father of all creation. That means that in time I will no longer look to other people to be the source of my self-esteem, security, or worth. I am sustained and validated by the Father of the universe, who has His plan and purpose for my life—and that is all that matters. Who I know, and how they can influence or control my life, is no longer an issue. I am free to trust God to bring the people into my life who will further His plans for me—and them! I become free to give and receive love, support, encouragement, and help without condition, restraint, or anxiety. We learn the pecking order in elementary school—who is important to hang out with and who is social suicide. We learn to calculate, manipulate, and operate each other to jockey for social status, public approval, and sadly, even our sense of self-worth.

My girlfriend Leeann suggested it was easy to tell how "cool" someone felt in high school by which Beatle she fantasized about. The pretty girls went for Paul, the popular ones for John, the smart ones for George, and everyone else settled for Ringo. But we don't need to fantasize about having a real relationship with the *coolest* person in the universe—God Almighty! With Him as our best friend, we don't have to worry about how cool anyone else is or how cool anyone else thinks we are. We are hanging out with the Almighty, and no one can have a greater influence on our lives than He does.

Let's face it—getting involved with other people is messy, risky business. We worry that if we commit to helping others, they may need us forever or drain us dry or just use us. We become resentful when they do not appreciate what we've done, or reciprocate. We also worry that if we allow ourselves to depend on someone, we may become weak and vulnerable. But when we trust that God has purposefully joined us *and* our needs together, we can relax and become generous givers and gracious receivers.

Jesus told the story of a Samaritan man who one day came upon a wounded traveler lying by the side of the road. Others hurried by the injured man, trying to ignore his need, but the Samaritan, a man whose culture was despised by the Jews, stopped to help the stranger. He tended to his wounds, provided for his care, and even paid for his hotel stay while he was recuperating. Jesus said that we are to act toward others in the same way as this Samaritan.[19] No doubt he had other plans that day. No doubt he felt insecure and uneasy caring for someone who under other circumstances would be judgmental and perhaps even hostile toward him. It may have even entered the Samaritan's mind that this wounded man probably would never have stopped to help him if the circumstances were reversed. But the Samaritan let God interrupt his agenda, his preferences, his plans for a more important purpose. God has a purpose of blessing for the people He puts in our lives.

ABILITIES

When we surrender our agendas to God, we must also surrender our abilities, talents, gifts, skills, and preferences for Him to develop for His pleasure and purpose. Our accomplishments are no longer as important as reflecting His love and glorifying His magnificence in every aspect of our lives. Some people believe that there is a difference in how and what we commit to in the "secular" world versus what we do and how we act in the context of the "Christian" world. We tend to adjust our behaviors, attitudes, and even language depending on whether we are in a church environment or the "real world." To God, there is only *one* world—His! There is no division for Him. Every corner of the earth is His, and every circumstance is an opportunity for us to spread His Kingdom of redemptive love to glorify His mighty name. No matter what venue we are in, we are in God's domain. Butcher, baker, candlestick maker—we are here to serve His purposes, and His purposes are not just found in churches. God wants to use every gift, every ability, every talent and passion He has given us—wherever we are, no matter whom we are with. Our business sense is as useful to the church as it is to our employer. Kindness is as important in the office as it is in Sunday school. God wants to use our

abilities in ways we can hardly imagine, to accomplish more than we
could dream. But God doesn't operate on a five-day workweek or an
eight-hour day! He wants us to be available for Him to use 24-7, in
every situation, for every opportunity.

Paul wrote:

> In his grace, God has given us different gifts for doing
> certain things well. So if God has given you the ability
> to prophesy, speak out with as much faith as God has
> given you. If your gift is serving others, serve them well.
> If you are a teacher, teach well. If your gift is to encour-
> age others, be encouraging. If it is giving, give gener-
> ously. If God has given you leadership ability, take the
> responsibility seriously. And if you have a gift for show-
> ing kindness to others, do it gladly.[20]

Surrendering our abilities means we allow God to use us in unexpected ways, at unexpected times. It means committing to develop
and grow in our areas of competence and accepting that God can be
very creative in how He uses us. My husband never thought that God
would use his civil engineer training to design a tent city in Mexico
for schoolkids on a mission trip. But what an adventure that turned
out to be! My friend Lisa has a passion and ability for quilting, and
God has a passion for sending quilts to orphans around the world.
When Lisa's quilting group donated a dozen or so quilts to a mission
team going to Africa, they never dreamed that they were starting a
major ministry. They just wanted God to use the fruits of their labors.

EMOTIONS

When we begin to surrender every area to God's agenda, one of the
greatest surprises is that we are no longer helpless against our emotions and impulses. We can discipline ourselves to choose how we

respond to events and circumstances. Although I still may tend to see the glass as half empty, because I trust that God has a better plan for what my glass is going to hold, I have the power to choose hope instead of despair, anticipation instead of anxiety.

When we accept Jesus as Lord of our lives, we receive the gift of the Spirit of God in our very beings. "Your body is the temple of the Holy Spirit, who lives in you and was given to you by God."[21] The amazing thing is, the more we surrender to God's plan, the more the Holy Spirit will begin to influence our choices and character. He is our helper and the power that God gives us for living out His plans. The Holy Spirit doesn't change who we are. Instead, He empowers us to become who we were created to be. He frees us from the enticements of the world around us, as well as our past patterns, bad habits, and negative attitudes.

In the past, I always allowed my insecurities to get the better of my feelings. If Greg commented on how nice I looked, I assumed that what he really meant was that I looked worse yesterday. A compliment on dinner was just his way of telling me that my cooking usually stank. I have been accused of looking for the storm behind every rainbow! One day, after yet another bout of tears over my misinterpretation of his comments, Greg sat me down and tenderly said, "Robyn, if there are two ways to interpret a comment from me—a positive way and a negative way—isn't it just as easy to assume I mean it the positive way?" Greg helped me realize that I have a choice over my feelings. Just because I have always seen the glass as cracked doesn't mean I have to believe it's leaking too! I can choose to start listening to the Holy Spirit instead of my insecurities. I can choose to break those patterns of seeing and hearing things in the negative and replace them with a new, positive outlook. We are no longer controlled by our sinful natures. We can become increasingly empowered by the Spirit if we have the Spirit of God living in us.[22]

The more influence we allow the Holy Spirit to have over our personalities and characters, the more God changes us. We can see the events of our lives and our world from a new perspective, and we are able to respond to them in a new way—a way distinguished by compassion and love, self-control and joy. Instead of feeling hopeless or frustrated by the daily headlines, we begin to respond to the events of our world as cries for prayer, opportunities to help, and possibilities for reconciliation. We can choose not to "copy the behavior and customs of this world, but let God transform you into a new person by changing the way you think. Then you will learn to know God's will for you, which is good and pleasing and perfect."[23]

Ironically, letting go of our feeble attempts to stay in control allows us to have fuller command of our choices. When we recognize that it is God who brings the people, events, and opportunities into our lives, then regardless of how we feel, we can *choose* to respond with obedience to His will and with thanksgiving for the goodness of that will. In all areas, letting go of my agenda and allowing God to take control produces joy in my life!

QUESTIONS

How does the concept of surrendering every part of your life to God make you feel?

Relieved, it is awesome to know I am a child of the most high God & he will take care of me no matter what.

What area of your life do you have the most difficulty giving up to God's control: your relationships, your abilities, your emotions, or something else?

Relationships definitely. I want love so bad that it is hard for me to wait for the person God has in mind. $ is another area that is hard for me.

What changes do you think would happen in the way you live your life if you were to begin surrendering those areas to God's agenda instead of pursuing your plans, dreams, and desires? I don't think that I would be worried as much about the future, because I would be constantly reassured that God will lead me where he wants me.

Take a few moments to prayerfully consider the events of your life in the last twenty-four hours. How might you have acted differently if you believed that God had orchestrated, purposed, and intentionally planned every encounter with every person you had contact with during your day? I may be more humble w/ judging others @ work, I may judge positively instead of always negatively. Maybe I wouldn't lead Jon on even though I do still miss him & have feelings for him. I need to thank God for these people I have contact w/ & not cut them down. They were made in his image too! ☺

How might you have responded differently if you had realized that God had allowed every event in your day as an opportunity for you to use your gifts and abilities for His Kingdom's glory? Maybe try to be more understanding of people that I don't get along w/ real well in the office. Care about others instead of the constant "ME, ME, ME!"

✱ *Consider what it means to glorify God with your life.*✱

Understand that he knows whats best for me & he is my shepherd. I should be more positive & encourage people when they say that they are struggling w/ things. Be patient when it comes to my future. Allow God to have complete control over my life.

3

Embrace Reality

FACING WHAT IS

No eye has seen, no ear has heard, and no mind has imagined
what God has prepared for those who love him.
1 CORINTHIANS 2:9

THE REAL WORLD

Where God leads, God provides! Shortly after we received the gift of
Michelle, we contacted a leading plastic surgeon in Denver. We had
heard that he was the best. Little did we know that his *specialty* was
cleft lip and cleft palate repair and that in fact he had devised his own
technique and procedures that yielded amazing results—both aes-
thetically and functionally. He wanted Michelle to weigh eight
pounds before surgery; it took almost four months to get her just
under the desired weight.

Meanwhile, Greg and I were experiencing the overflow of God's
blessings. Not only was our tiny daughter the light of our lives, but six
weeks after she came home, we got a call from Lutheran Social Services. I had actually forgotten about the pending Filipino program we
had applied for during those frantic pre-Michelle days. But there they
were on the phone, telling us that they were ready to start the procedure for adoption. When I explained that although we did want more

children eventually, we had just adopted a baby and weren't quite ready to adopt again, the voice on the phone assured me that we would remain "number one" on their waiting list. I was to give them a call when we were ready for baby number two.

One year and two surgeries later, we gave them a call. We were ready for a son! They told us that a little boy had just been born with a cleft lip and cleft palate, and his young mother was anxious for him to be placed as soon as possible, preferably with an American family. Were we interested? Three months later, Joshua Marc came home to us. We named him Joshua, "Jehovah saves," and kept his original name, Marc, for his middle name—a name that would later confirm God's call on his life.

With the false confidence that comes from being the parents of one, Greg and I picked up our tiny, almost four-month-old son from the airport with utter assurance in our parenting skills. We had already dealt with the physical and emotional issues that come with babies and cleft lip/palate surgeries, so we felt quite sure that we had a handle on this parenting thing. We stopped at my parents' house on the way home from the airport so Joshua could meet Grammy and Papa. My mother was walking home from work when we drove up, and as if he knew that this was his grandmother, Joshua began bouncing on my lap when he saw her and broke forth with a smile that lit up the car. Little did we suspect that would be the last smile we would see for a long time.

By the time we got him home that evening he had begun to get fussy—nothing unusual for a baby who had traveled halfway around the world. But his fussy night turned into a fussy week, then month, then three months. Though he continued to grow, he didn't develop skills at a normal rate—in fact, developmentally he seemed stalled. He cried, or more accurately, screamed and thrashed, for hours on end. The doctor told us he was having difficulty bonding, and then we were told he was colicky.

Three months after he arrived, he had his first surgery. Even the nurses commented on what an unhappy baby he was. He cried so persistently that he popped one of his lip-repair stitches. Nothing made him happy; nothing soothed him. He seemed to be in pain, yet there were no symptoms of injury or illness. And so he cried. And cried. And cried.

And when he wasn't crying, he was screaming. Often when Greg got home at the end of the day I would leave to "run errands"—really just an excuse to get away for a while. I discovered an affection for grocery stores that were miles away, just to extend my travel time! On the weekends Greg would take over Joshua's care to give me a break. Greg has always been a calming, patient, and positive influence in my life, and during this time I realized even more what a treasure God had blessed me with in my husband. It was during this time that "Mom's night off" began in our home. Every Thursday, as soon as he got home from the office, Greg would take over for the whole evening—making dinner, giving baths, tucking the kids in bed—while I got the night off. Since I was usually way too exhausted to actually go out, I would retire to the bedroom with a book and enjoy a bubble bath and relatively quiet solitude for the evening. Heaven on earth!

When Joshua was nine months old, a lump developed on his neck. It turned out to be a rare form of tuberculosis that affects the lymph nodes. After medication failed, the diseased lymph nodes were surgically removed. And still he cried and failed to develop—"failure to thrive," we were told. Why, we didn't know.

At almost a year old he had his third surgery, to repair his palate. And still he cried. He wasn't crawling or babbling; by now his progress was becoming seriously delayed. We thought perhaps his problem was allergies, so we cut out milk products, then soy products, then wheat, then sugars, then processed foods. We were desperate for anything that would stop his discomfort. We couldn't hold him; he would thrash and fling himself backward when we tried to cuddle or nurture him.

Thankfully, Michelle was a quick, delightful, affectionate child who was developing into a bright and beautiful little girl. At barely two years old, she adapted quickly to her brother's arrival and temperament as she helped care for him.

The crying was heartbreaking; we loved this baby so much. Before Joshua arrived I used to worry that I might not be able to love another child as much as I loved Michelle. I imagined ridiculous scenarios about what I would do if both my children's safety was threatened—whom would I save first, or which one would I save if I could save only one? Shortly after Joshua arrived, we were in the car, both of my babies in their car seats, when the car next to me suddenly and inexplicably veered into my lane. Panicked, I swerved onto the shoulder of the road, barely missing being hit. I pulled off the road still shaking, imagining what could have happened. Suddenly I had to start chuckling. I realized that if both my children were threatened, I wouldn't choose which one to save; I would die trying to save both! They were (and still are) my heart, my breath, my joy, my life. Yet I could not soothe this baby. I could not comfort him. Why?

Joshua turned a year old at the end of June 1977. He was seriously delayed. Five months later, in November, after he had been with us for a full year, he woke up one morning and didn't cry! I went to pick him up, change him, and feed him—still no crying. I put him on the floor, and Michelle and I began to play with him—no crying. At nap time he sat on my lap next to Michelle, and we read a book. No crying, no thrashing about, and he actually snuggled next to me. When Greg walked in the house from work, a new sensation met his ears—quiet! He must have thought he had accidentally walked into the wrong house. The sounds of my cooking dinner and the babies—*both of them*—playing in the kitchen were truly the heavenly sounds of a gift from God!

One day turned into two, and we held our breath. How long would this last? Then a week, then a month . . . blessed relief, it was over. Several months later, our pediatrician called to suggest a theory. He had just received an article published by the American Medical Association regarding babies who had been born addicted to drugs. Joshua displayed all the symptoms. After some research and testing, it was determined that our little boy had been born addicted—most likely to heroin. Not only did Joshua endure the torture of heroin withdrawal, but the doctor also surmised that his delicate little system couldn't properly process the additional drugs he had been given during his surgeries. The resulting physical and emotional distress was responsible for his failure to develop and bond properly. None of us were sure what long-term effects we might face. We were just thankful that he was finally happy.

Joshua's development was amazing, and he soon made up for lost time. God promised to "give you back what you lost,"[1] and He did! It quickly became apparent that we had an exceptionally bright, talented son with an abundance of energy and imagination. (That's a mother's way of saying that he was quite a handful.) Joshua began to test limits almost as soon as he was aware that there were such things. If a line was drawn, he was sure to cross it. As he got older, his antics became increasingly dangerous. No tree was too tall to climb and then *jump from*. No window was too precarious to climb out of or sneak back in through. He was labeled "strong-willed," and desperately trying to "tame" our energetic young son, I mistakenly and tragically followed the Christian pop psychology of the times: tough love, unshakable boundaries, and a firm hand. This was terrible advice for loving a child with emotional baggage, insecurity, and borderline social dysfunction. I succeeded only in confirming his feelings of inadequacy, damaging his fragile self-identity, and leaving him wounded.

Joshua would later confide to me that all his young life he *knew* he was different. To a child, different means bad, and it feels wrong.

Joshua knew that he saw things from a different perspective from most other people; he felt things more intensely, and he imagined things more vividly. He didn't measure up (or down) to the norm.

A verse from Proverbs (misinterpreted) was the motto of "Christian" parenting and the justification for trying to pour our children into inflexible molds: "Train a child in the way he should go, and when he is old he will not turn from it."[2] The idea was that as parents, it is our responsibility to mold every thought, attitude, dream, and goal for our kids. If we make our rules firm enough, our kids will turn out just the way we planned! If we establish our expectations for them solidly enough, they will live up to our dreams. If our reins are tight enough, our children will never rebel or embarrass us or get out of control. The problem with this philosophy is that it leaves no room for the individuality God created in our children, the imagination He intended to use in them, or the energy He wanted to tap into. The truth of this proverb is that as parents we should discover and encourage our children's God-given identity so that when they grow up they will be confident in their calling.

Years later, I had the opportunity to apologize to my gracious and forgiving son for my hurtful parenting methods. I loved him with a resolute intensity but likewise feared for his future. I was afraid that *I* would somehow fail to be a good mother and that it would be my inadequacy that would cause him to make dreadful choices and fall into terrible mistakes. I thought Joshua's future depended upon my perfection as a parent, instead of God's guidance. I tried to control what God intended to be free. I realize now that my greatest sin as Joshua's mother was to know more about what the Christian psychologists of the day had to say than I knew about what God had to say. I read and followed parenting books more faithfully than I did the Word of God! I let the "experts" tell me what God had to say instead of listening to Him myself. And I tried to make Josh fit into their molds instead of helping him to grow into the child God had created him to be.

The sin of a fallen world and the drug abuse of his birth mother—no doubt a wounded young soul herself—had physically damaged Joshua's infant body, but my sin damaged his soul. Joshua's young life would be lived with a self-destructive vengeance. His infancy was but the first of many storms we would face in his life. But the storm will bring blessing—eventually! However, the storm must first be faced. We must accept and confront the reality of our situation.

"The truth *will* set you free"[3]—free from the fantasy "should haves" and "what ifs" of our futile plans and schemes. But we can be free only when we fully face how things *really are*—not how we want them to be, how we remember them to be, or even how we claim them to be. We must embrace reality—all of its fact, emotion, and effort—and claim it as the condition of our lives. Then we give it to God for Him to use, mold, and perfect for His purposes.

EMBRACING REALITY

It is *today* that God wants to bless, and it is *now* that God wants to use. But He will use only the truth of today, not our fantasies, our illusions, or the culturally or politically correct descriptions of what is happening in our lives. It is important for us to accept our actual condition emotionally, relationally, physically, and spiritually. Many factors distort our comprehension of reality. We see our lives through the context of our cultural and ethical standards, our beliefs, and our past. But if we want to be in a place of blessing, if we want to experience the fullness that God has for us, we need to be fully present in the reality of our *today*.

RELEASE THE PAST

Our perception of the past has much to do with our perspective of the present. The fact is that often our memories taint (or at least tint) the events of our past. Nothing demonstrates that better than sitting around the kitchen table with grown-up siblings, reliving past adventures. Several years ago, all our grown children came home for the Christmas holidays. In the evenings we always ended up around the kitchen table, usually along with a fair amount of food, some sort of board game, and plenty of laughter. Sooner or later, someone would start remembering a particularly exciting adventure from their childhood (the more it scared or shocked Mom the better, of course). It was amazing how many versions of one story came out! And of course, Dad and Mom remembered the events entirely differently than the kids did. What one child remembers as fun, another remembers as scary or boring or stupid—and of course someone else doesn't even remember it happening.

Our memories are rarely totally accurate. They are colored by the emotional, relational, physical, psychological, spiritual, and even political and cultural conditions we were experiencing at the time. They are further altered by the events that preceded and followed each memory, by our perspective of the event—whether we were involved or just witnessing—and by our ability to understand and process what was happening. A five-year-old and a ten-year-old will certainly remember the same event differently, for example. Nothing illustrates this better than our recollections of major news events that have happened in our own lifetimes. I was in junior high when President Kennedy was assassinated. My memories of the event revolve around losing a personal hero, whereas my parents' memories were from the perspective of losing a national leader. My little sister, who was barely five at the time, remembers it only as a historical event. The impact of those memories helped shape my political sensibilities as I got older. I embraced what I considered to be the causes of my fallen hero. On the other hand, for my little sister, those memories had little personal impact. The experiences of our past profoundly affect our lives, but they must not be allowed to control or distort our perception of our present reality. Political issues in 1963 really were different from what is happening today, and although I am still committed to many of my original causes, I have had to realize that they call for different solutions in the new millennium.

Some of us have been severely damaged by events or people, and it is imperative that we take the necessary therapeutic steps to bring healing and wholeness and forgiveness into our pain. We must not allow the past to prevent us from receiving what God wants to give us today—His blessing, His power, and His grace.

The apostle Paul had a terrible history to overcome. He brutalized believers of Christ; by his own admission he "violently persecuted God's church," even "hounding some to death, arresting both men and women and throwing them in prison."[4] But by the grace of God, Paul found the key to allowing God to use his present as fully as possible:

> I focus on this one thing: Forgetting the past and looking
> forward to what lies ahead, I press on to reach the end of
> the race and receive the heavenly prize for which God,
> through Christ Jesus, is calling us.[5]

We have to deal with the past once and for all. We must allow God to heal the hurts, bring restoration, and release us from the effects of the memories so that He can move us onward for His purposes. We must realize that God wants to bring us to a new and effective time and place in our lives. God told Israel, "Forget the former things; do not dwell on the past. See, I am doing a new thing! Now it springs up; do you not perceive it?"[6]

If we allow Him to, God will use our past *today* to bless our lives and the lives of others through us. The Bible tells us to praise God, the Father of our Lord Jesus Christ, because He is the source of every mercy. He is the God who wants to comfort us in all our troubles so that we can comfort others in the same way. When others face the same troubles we have faced, we are able to show them God's mercy because we have already experienced it.[7] That is one of the ways God will bring good from our hard times.[8] When we release our past to God—allowing His power to use, heal, restore, set right, and give us clarity for today—we put ourselves in a place of blessing. Whenever we bring any part of ourselves into His Kingdom, we can be confident that He will never waste it. It will become a source of blessing for us as well as through us, for others.

RELINQUISH TODAY

The greatest barrier to releasing our dreams, decisions, and plans to God is fear. It is simplistic to say that fear is no more than a lack of trust in God; our fears are often based on very real experiences and pain. We know what it is like to fail, to be at the mercy of the unknown, to disappoint and be disappointed. We bear the scars of damaged lives existing in a fallen world. We have all tasted the bitter judgment of being misunderstood or rejected. It is hard to let go of our fears, to trust in an unknown future, to abandon what little power we believe we have over our lives. Yet the greatest power we will ever experience is the power of letting go and allowing God to become more and more the center of our choices, decisions, and priorities.

Throughout the Bible God tells us, "Fear not, for . . ." Fear not, *for!* *For* I am with you, *for* I will protect you, *for* I will strengthen you, *for* I will give you victory, *for* I hear you. God does not condemn our fear; He comforts, strengthens, guides, and helps us *in* our fear. To face our fears and proceed *anyway*—that is trust, that is faith, that is the power of God's grace in our lives. (For a partial list of the more than 365 "fear not" statements in the Bible, see appendix C.)

God says to His people, to those who are willing to trust Him:

> Do not be afraid, for I have ransomed you. I have called
> you by name; you are mine. When you go through deep

waters, I will be with you. When you go through rivers
of difficulty, you will not drown. When you walk
through the fire of oppression, you will not be burned
up; the flames will not consume you. For I am the LORD,
your God, the Holy One of Israel, your Savior. . . . You
are precious to me. You are honored, and I love you.[9]

Through trouble, difficulty, oppression, and whatever circumstances this world brings, God is there. He is waiting for us to turn to
Him and follow Him through the anxieties, sorrows, and dangers to
safety and victory. Fear not! Relinquish the fear of the unknown; we
have no *real* control over our future anyway. Fear not! Relinquish the
fear of failure; there is no victory more complete than His. Fear not!
Relinquish the fear of rejection; He will never reject us. God tells us
that He has even engraved us on the palms of His hands.[10] Fear not!
Relinquish the fear of pain; He will comfort us and then turn our pain
into blessing. God tells us not to be afraid. Fear not, just for today!
Dare to sample what God has in store for you today. "No eye has
seen, no ear has heard, and no mind has imagined what God has prepared for those who love him."[11]

As a young girl, I often thought that I could never bear it if I could
not have children. I was afraid that my dreams would not come true.
But God had a bigger dream for my childbearing. He wanted to give
me children I never could have had on my own.

As a young woman, I thought that I could *never* mother a child with
disabilities. I was afraid that I couldn't handle the difficulty. But God
had a bigger dream for my motherhood. He wanted to bless my socks
off by showing me new worlds of "capabilities" that I never could have
imagined.

There is a difference between simply being aware of the condition of
my life and submitting those conditions to be used for God's purposes.
There is a difference between simply accepting my circumstances and

offering those circumstances as potential for God's glory. There is a difference between simply adjusting to my situation and expecting the abundance of God's blessing and goodness to come from that situation. To live God's dream for our *today*, we must bravely move beyond awareness, acceptance, and adjustment to an attitude of submission, offering, and expectant trust in God's great dream for today!

REALIGN THE PRESENT

God wants to bless our lives. He wants to use our today. He wants us to live today for Him and His purposes. How do we interpret whether the conditions and circumstances of our lives are on course with His purposes? What criteria do we use? We must have some idea of whether we are on His course or our own "crash course."

If we are going to embrace the reality of God's plan for us, we must acknowledge the real condition of our lives. The Word and will of God are the foundational standards of our moral integrity, our cultural ethics, our personal legacy, and our significance—not societal standards or our own feelings and opinions. Any standards outside of God's lack the eternal and timeless perspective of God and therefore are flawed and skewed. If we desire to live a significant and blessed life, we must live the kind of life that God blesses: a life based on His truth, in obedience to His will, and available for His use. That means we must hold up our lives to the revealing light of God's truth. It means we must stop making excuses for our actions and justifying our attitudes—and instead live in the light of openness and accountability to God's Word.

To fully comprehend the context of the circumstances we encounter, we must also be aware that our lives are part of God's eternal plan and purposes. All history has its beginning and will have its eventual ending in God's will and plan. Each life has been planned and purposed by God. Psalm 139 tells us that God knit us together and knew us even while we were being formed in our mother's womb. And Ephesians 1:11 says that we were a part of God's plan from the very beginning. Now that's significance! We are not accidents. God created each one of us for two reasons: for Him to love us and for us to be valued and precious components of His Kingdom. No matter our strengths and weaknesses, our abilities and needs, our aptitudes and limitations, our advantages and disadvantages, our past and present circumstances—we are here by God's planning. God has a purpose and use for us now—today—where we are emotionally, physically, and circumstantially, for just this time and in just this place![12]

We live in the context of God's unchanging standard of love and goodness and within His continually unfolding design. Our greatest significance can be realized only when we accept that we are a part of that plan. Our dreams and desires are minuscule compared to God's. Our achievements, no matter how grandiose, are minute compared to what God can accomplish in, through, and with our lives. When we begin to realize how important each day is, how significant every decision and every choice, we begin to grasp how crucial it is to base our lives on something more substantial than feelings and more reliable than chance. God wants for us lives of truly lasting and eternal accomplishment. But before we can take full advantage of His will for us, we must determine to see our lives as they really are—from His perspective, so we can set our course by His compass.

OBEDIENCE

To embrace the purpose, potential, and blessing of our lives, we must be centered on God's presence and within the context of His will. We must be intentional about seeking Him and determined to follow Him. We must be intentional about knowing His will and determined to live in accordance with that will. God has given us His written guidebook, the Bible. Through His holy and living Word, we can know how God has designed us and what His plans are for our lives. It is the owner's manual and instructional guide for our "optimum running conditions." But the simple fact is, the manual is of no value if it is left unread. To do the will of God, we must know the Word of God. It does not matter what we *think* God wants, how we *feel* about God's desires for us, or what our *opinions* are about God's commands. The truth is found in one place only: His Word.

The psalmist declared that God's Word is "a lamp to guide my feet and a light for my path."[13] It shines a light on our circumstances and exposes them in relation to God's plans, and it clarifies our decisions by illuminating the priorities and actions that will eventually lead to God's blessing. Obedience is a choice based on intent and action. First we intentionally become familiar with what God wants for us, and then we take the necessary action to bring our lives into alignment with Him.

In the evenings, Greg and I like to walk around a nearby lake. Over the years, we have become familiar with each other's gait and style of walking. Greg, who is a natural runner, walks with purpose and direction. I, on the other hand, tend to stroll, wandering off on the side paths to check out the duck families or to see what plants are blooming. Walking *together* is the joy, so we intentionally have become familiar with each other's styles. We frequently make adjustments to our pace in order to keep in step with each other. Over the years this time together has become more and more precious and intimate. Obedience to God is in many ways the same. Over time, through intentional attention and frequent adjustments we become familiar with His pace, and our journey becomes more and more intimate.

We obey God by choosing to admit when we have challenged His ways and will in thought, word, deed, or attitude. That's called *confession*—agreeing with God that we are outside His design. And we obey God when we intend with all our willingness and all our commitment to follow *His* ways from now on. That's called *repentance*—exchanging our ways, the world's ways, and society's ways for God's ways.

Jesus said:

> Those who accept my commandments and obey them
> are the ones who love me. And because they love me,
> my Father will love them. And I will love them and *reveal*
> myself to each of them. . . . All who love me will do
> what I say. My Father will love them, and we will *come*
> *and make our home with each of them.*[14]

Living the way God desires us to live allows us to see Jesus more clearly and to experience His presence and power more fully in our lives. Obedience places us in a position of blessing and usefulness for God. We obey not out of fear of God's rejection or in an attempt to earn God's love. In fact, true obedience of heart, mind, and action is something we cannot even do on our own. The apostle Paul wrote:

> The sinful nature wants to do evil, which is just the
> opposite of what the Spirit wants. And the Spirit gives us
> desires that are the opposite of what the sinful nature
> desires. These two forces are constantly fighting each
> other, so you are not free to carry out your good inten-
> tions. But when you are directed by the Spirit, you are
> not under obligation to the law of Moses.[15]

The Old Testament law represents God's intention for our lives; it illustrates holiness lived out and characterizes a God-directed life. The Old Testament established the means by which an imperfect person could maintain a relationship with a perfect God. But now that we have the Holy Spirit (God's Spirit in us, available through our belief in Christ's sacrifice), the law is no longer the foundation for our continued relationship with God. In fact, all the demands of that law have already been fully met for us by Christ. Jesus said, "Don't misun-derstand why I have come. I did not come to abolish the law of Moses or the writings of the prophets. No, I came to accomplish their

purpose."[16] Romans 3:25 explains that Christ fulfilled the require-
ments of God's holy law by suffering the consequences for our sins.
That is why those who have been saved by Christ no longer need the
law for salvation. Once we possess the Holy Spirit, the very Spirit of
that law of holiness exists in our inner beings. He leads, directs, and
corrects us from within. So obedience to God's will—living according
to God's intentions for our lives—is not about outward effort. Instead,
it is achieved by spiritual submission, or acquiescing our will for God's
will in us. Ultimately, it is only by our faith that we are able to live in
accordance with God's plan for us.[17]

God lovingly wants to use our lives for His good purposes and for
His abundant blessings, no matter where we are right now or what we
are experiencing. But we must be in a place of blessing, an attitude of
compliance. God will not intrude on our lives. He has given us the
choice! The Bible challenges and warns us:

> Don't you realize that you become the slave of whatever
> you choose to obey? You can be a slave to sin, which
> leads to death, or you can choose to obey God, which
> leads to righteous living.[18]
>
> Choose today whom you will serve.[19]

Today is the day to choose. Today is the time God wants to use. He
has a dream for you today! God's blessings are part of the real world,
and we need to fully invest our attention, time, and energy to what is
really happening. We need to take the steps to accept reality, to realize that we are part of a bigger plan, and to trust our lives to His
design.

QUESTIONS

Prayerfully spend a few moments reflecting on the following Scripture passage:

> O LORD, you have examined my heart and know every-
> thing about me. . . . Search me, O God, and know my
> heart; test me and know my anxious thoughts. Point out
> anything in me that offends you, and lead me along the
> path of everlasting life. PSALM 139:1, 23-24

*Using this passage, ask God to reveal any past circumstance, hurt, or event that has
hindered you from fully embracing the potential that He wants for you today. Ask
God to help you release those memories or events to His cleansing, His forgiveness,
His healing, and His use.*

*Using the same passage, ask God to examine your perception of your present. Ask
Him to reveal any areas in your priorities, attitudes, or behavior that are contrary to
His will. Consider what steps you need to take to bring those areas into alignment
with God's plan for your life.*

*Is there an area of your life that you need to confess (agree with God that you are
outside His will)?*

Is there any attitude or practice for which you need to repent (exchange your way for God's way)?

In what areas of your life do you struggle the most with fear (e.g., uncertainty about the future, failure, criticism, inadequacy, abandonment)?

How would knowing that God wants to provide for you in your fear and use and bless that very area of your life change the way you act or think?

Ask God to help you write a simple "Fear not, for I am . . ." promise that deals with that area of your life. For ideas, read through the list of "Fear Not" statements in appendix C. Spend some time prayerfully meditating on the promise you wrote.

4

*See from
God's Heart*

CHANGING PERSPECTIVE

Blessed is she who has believed that what the Lord has said
to her will be accomplished!
LUKE 1:45 (NIV)

BLESSED TO BELIEVE

In 1975 we adopted Michelle, God's gift from Vietnam. In 1976 we adopted Joshua, God's blessing from the Philippines. In 1978 we went back to our county agency. Several years had passed, we were older, and we already had two special-needs children of other races, so we felt that surely we would *now* qualify for an older special-needs child from our own state. Were we in for a rude awakening! We were told by the head of the county social services department that because we had brought non-American children into our home, we were no longer "worthy" of county placement. It was God's way of closing that door to us, forever.

In January 1979 we got a call from the head of Lutheran Social Services. There was a baby girl in Seoul, Korea, with a cleft lip and cleft palate. Were we interested? We couldn't say yes fast enough. The paperwork took more than three months to process, and it was late April when our little Nori came home, at just over a year old.

We arrived at the airport plenty early. Meeting new children at Stapleton Airport had become a regular drill in our lives. Over the last few years we had developed friendships with many other adoptive families, and picking up our new additions at the airport was a joy we shared with our friends. We also had begun hosting children who had overnight travel layovers in Denver. We would pick them up at the airport in the evening, then the next morning put them on a connecting flight that would take them to their adoptive families. Over the years we had dozens of children stay with us. By the time Michelle was four and Joshua was three, we realized that they were getting a rather unique perspective of life. When another child asked them if they knew where babies came from, Michelle answered definitively, "Babies come from the airport. Girls come from United and boys come from American!"

So it was with great joy and expectation that our friends joined us that morning at Stapleton Airport to welcome home our new baby girl. We waited impatiently as the plane disembarked. The arriving children were almost always the last off, but finally we saw her—a tiny bundle in her escort's arms, sleeping quietly. We had already known about her severe bilateral cleft lip and cleft palate, but that seemed to be the least of her problems. Even before we left the airport, we realized that there was something very different about this child. She was limp and unresponsive. *Jet lag*, I decided. *She's just exhausted.* We stopped briefly at Grammy and Papa's house on our way home from the airport. My mother's first response was, "Look at her darling hands. She has such gentle, delicate, expressive hands." Prophetic words, as it turned out, for her sweet, tiny hands would eventually be the key to unlocking this quiet, closed rosebud.

The first days after her arrival, I tried to convince myself, and everyone who came to see her, that our poor baby was just exhausted. "It's a long flight from Korea, you know!" I would say. But it soon became apparent that there was something much, much more serious about her behavior—or, really, lack of behavior. She was over thirteen months old, yet she couldn't hold up her head or roll over. She was unresponsive to noise or touch—in fact, when we tried to interact with her in any way, she would fall into a deep sleep, from which she could not be aroused. She never made eye contact; she never made *any* sound. No babbling, laughing, smiling, or even crying. In fact, the only thing she did was hypnotically wiggle her little sweet fingers in front of her face, side to side, every waking minute of her day. She was virtually impossible to feed because she would immediately drop off into a deep sleep if I touched her! By the time we took her to her first pediatrician's appointment, I was starting to feel despair creeping in. *What could possibly be wrong with our daughter?*

Our doctor confirmed our worst fears. Nori was severely and probably irreparably delayed—physically, intellectually, and emotionally. She weighed barely twelve pounds at thirteen months old and appeared to have symptoms of severe autism. We were encouraged to try to "return her" before we became attached. The doctor clearly didn't understand adoption, which is a process not dissimilar to pregnancy. When a mother first finds out that she is expecting a child, she begins to dream about who that child will be, what she will look like, how their life together will play out. As the time of arrival approaches, the maternal feeling of bonding has already developed. The sense of belonging—she to the child and the child to her—is already formed, even though mother and child have yet to actually meet each other. This is true regardless of how the child arrives. With pregnancy or adoption, by the time the child is in her mother's arms, the child is already hers, and the mother is already attached.

It was too late for me not to feel attached to this child; she was my daughter! Yet I was afraid. Afraid to freely love her, afraid of what pain her life might hold, afraid that I could not love her the way she deserved.

But I struggled with something far more destructive than my fear:

rage. Rage at God. Rage at the cruel hoax He had played on us.
Months before we heard about Nori, Greg and I had attended a
renewal retreat sponsored by our church. It was there that we both
recommitted our lives to Jesus Christ. It was there that we both
became stunningly aware of a depth of relationship with our Father in
heaven that we had never before known was possible. Some called it a
"born again" experience, but Scripture tells us that it is when we *first*
give our lives to Christ that we are born again.

> Jesus replied, "I tell you the truth, unless you are born
> again, you cannot see the Kingdom of God. . . . I assure
> you, no one can enter the Kingdom of God without
> being born of water and the Spirit. Humans can repro-
> duce only human life, but the Holy Spirit gives birth to
> spiritual life. So don't be surprised when I say, 'You must
> be born again.' . . . Everyone who believes in him will
> have eternal life. For God loved the world so much that
> he gave his one and only Son, so that everyone who
> believes in him will not perish but have eternal life."[1]

Greg and I had both committed our lives to Christ as children, but
this retreat showed us that we could have a new relationship, even an
intimate friendship and kinship, with Christ. We realized that it was
possible to live for and in the Kingdom of God right now, in this world.
And it was Good News indeed! Greg and I embraced our new relationship with our Lord and dedicated our lives to Him. So when Nori came,
with so many problems, I felt as if God had made me the butt of some
celestial practical joke. And I was *not* laughing! The psalmist cried out to
God, "You have made us the butt of their jokes."[2] That could have been
my theme song. I thought that turning our lives over to God meant
everything would be easy. Three easy steps to happiness, fulfillment,
security . . . you name it. After all, God rewards! I thought God did

nothing but good things—His gifts were always good. Didn't He say, "My yoke is easy to bear, and the burden I give you is light"?[3]

There was nothing easy or light about Nori's condition. And I raged. "God just couldn't be this mean. He wouldn't do something like this to us!" We had heard about Nori only a few months after our retreat, and we were convinced that God had led her to us. This was the daughter He intended for us—but we were not prepared for these circumstances.

I entered into the wonderful world of denial. *God wouldn't trick us this way*, I thought. *He knew that the one thing I had always said I could not handle was an intellectually challenged child, and therefore, this child just isn't going to be intellectually challenged!* So I denied the obvious. Nori was months behind in development; in fact, she completely failed the newborn tests. We were told that she had no natural responsive reflexes to noise, motion, or stimulation. She had no protective reflex. She had no apparent cognitive skills, no fine motor skills, no voluntary gross motor skills. She appeared to be deaf, and she had no developmental potential. But I was still convinced that it was just jet lag or delayed reflexes or any other invention I could think up. With a little time and energy, I would snap her out of it.

What followed could have been titled *The Exploits of a Maniacal Mom*. I would prop up the baby with pillows and roll a ball to her—which of course would immediately make her fall asleep to avoid the stimulation. I would surround her with toys and encourage her to "come get the doll," but all the while she was lying on her back, hypnotically wiggling her little fingers in front of her face. And inside, I would rage. Thoughts of the future were terrifying: I had visions of her at sixty and me in my eighties still trying to roll a ball to her. And most concerning of all, I truly did not want to love her—it just seemed too frightening, too painful. There were no good future options in sight; everything led only to heartbreak. How could I allow myself to be open to that?

Have you ever wondered why those really angry-sounding psalms ever made it into Scripture? I don't, not anymore. Those psalms became my prayer book during that period of my life. I was angry, and I felt as if God had purposely hurt me.

> I am worn out from sobbing. All night I flood my bed
> with weeping, drenching it with my tears. My vision is
> blurred by grief; my eyes are worn out because of all my
> enemies.[4]

> O LORD, I cry out to you. I will keep on pleading day by
> day. O LORD, why do you reject me? Why do you turn
> your face from me? I have been sick and close to death
> since my youth. I stand helpless and desperate before
> your terrors. Your fierce anger has overwhelmed me.
> Your terrors have paralyzed me. They swirl around me
> like floodwaters all day long. They have engulfed me
> completely. You have taken away my companions and
> loved ones. Darkness is my closest friend.[5]

Has anyone in the history of womankind ever been treated so poorly by God? I wondered. Yep, I took the pity party to new heights . . . and depths! If anyone had asked me if the sun had shone during those first few weeks with Nori, I would have honestly declared that it rained every day. Every day was gray, scary, and cold. But that was about to change.

God is a gentle and kind Father. He allows us our grief and self-pity . . . to a point. Then He lets us know that it's time to stop looking at ourselves and start looking up to Him and out to others. Several weeks after Nori arrived, I got a little note in the mail from the mother-in-law of my friend Kathy. She had been visiting Kathy and Tom the week Nori arrived, and she had seen our baby. She had even prayed with us over Nori, but I was still a bit surprised to see a note from her in my afternoon mail. Joshua and Michelle were in their rooms reading (an afternoon ritual at our house), and I sat down on the sofa to read the mail. At my feet, on a blanket, lying on her back, Nori was doing what she always did: waving her little hands in front of her face. I opened the note, and it read:

> Dear Robyn,
>
> I hope that you see progress in your little girl every day, but I pray that you will come to know that God has put her in your home so that she will become who He wants her to be.

I never saw this woman again, nor was I ever able to tell her how significant her words were. But somehow, I believe she knew that she was speaking from God's heart. If lightning had struck me in my family room that afternoon, it would not have had the impact of those words. I realized that I had been so busy trying to deny who Nori was and make her what *I* wanted her to be that I had never asked God to let me see who *He* had made her to be. I slid off the sofa and onto my knees, and this time I cried out to God with all my heart.

Forgive me! Forgive me for not seeing the gift of this child. Forgive me for trying to make her into my image of what I want her to be. Help me, Lord! Help me to love her! Help me to love her just the way she is!

It would not be the first or last time I would know that I was literally in the presence of God. A comforting inner warmth came over me, and I felt physically and emotionally embraced. Then I heard God's voice, clearly and unmistakably. I felt God telling me, **Child, you already love her! Do not be afraid to love her.**

With tears streaming down my face, I did the only thing that seemed natural. I lay down next to my baby and began to wiggle my fingers in front of my face. If she could not experience my world, I would experience hers!

It's amazing what peace can come from determining that my way *isn't* the only way. As I lay there next to this baby who had stolen my heart, I allowed myself to believe for the first time that her life was significant and valuable, regardless of what she would ever do—or not do. She was a child of God, created for the sole purpose of being loved by her Creator and bringing Him glory! If she never did *anything* but wiggle her fingers in front of her face, her life was precious and worthwhile. Those precious little hands of hers showed me the way to have a relationship with her—I could experience her world. And I would.

A few nights later, the doorbell rang at dinnertime. When we answered it, all that was there was a gift for me. It was a small plaque with a Bible verse on it: "Blessed is she who has believed that what the Lord has said to her will be accomplished!"[6]

Those words come from the mouth of Elizabeth, an older woman, barren—unable to have children—who found herself miraculously with child. Six months after Elizabeth became pregnant, God sent His angel Gabriel to Elizabeth's young virgin cousin Mary.

> Gabriel appeared to her and said, "Greetings, favored woman! The Lord is with you!" Confused and disturbed, Mary tried to think what the angel could mean. "Don't be afraid, Mary," the angel told her, "for you have found favor with God! You will conceive and give birth to a son, and you will name him Jesus. He will be very great and will be called the Son of the Most High. The Lord God will give him the throne of his ancestor David. And he will reign over Israel forever; his Kingdom will never end!" Mary asked the angel, "But how can this happen? I am a virgin." The angel replied, "The Holy Spirit will come upon you, and the power of the Most High will overshadow you. So the baby to be born will be holy, and he will be called the Son of God. What's more, your

relative Elizabeth has become pregnant in her old age!
People used to say she was barren, but she's now in her
sixth month. For nothing is impossible with God." Mary
responded, "I am the Lord's servant. May everything
you have said about me come true." And then the angel
left her.

The story continues:

A few days later Mary hurried to the hill country of
Judea, to the town where Zechariah lived. She entered
the house and greeted Elizabeth. At the sound of Mary's
greeting, Elizabeth's child [who would grow up to be
John the Baptist] leaped within her, and Elizabeth was
filled with the Holy Spirit. Elizabeth gave a glad cry and
exclaimed to Mary, "God has blessed you above all
women, and your child is blessed. Why am I so honored,
that the mother of my Lord should visit me? When I
heard your greeting, the baby in my womb jumped for
joy. *You are blessed because you believed that the Lord would do
what he said.*"[7]

I didn't know then why or how the verse on the plaque would apply
to me or my life, but it was a gift . . . a gift of hope. This verse would
become my "life verse," as God showed me over and over again that
His greatest blessing comes from *believing that what He has said and promised is true*.

I've learned many lessons from Nori's life, but the first one was to
accept gifts from God just *as He has given them*. Everything from God is a
gift to be received with open arms. It might not look or act the way we
had envisioned. It might not fit the mold of what we thought it should
be or what the world's standards say it should be. It may not have

come to us by the means we had hoped—no, it is better, it is divine, it is holy. We cannot look at gifts from God through the world's perspective. We need to train ourselves to see from God's heart!

SEEING FROM GOD'S HEART

God looked over all he had made, and he saw that it was very good![8]

Everything God gives is good, and everything that is good is from God—by definition. God *is* good! But we judge the goodness, validity, and worth of people, things, and events by a subjective standard. It's a measurement based largely on our own personal perceptions of value: the amount of comfort, contentment, potential, pleasure, accomplishment, prestige, power, and so forth that we can derive from that person, thing, or event. The problem with this measure is that we end up missing out on many (maybe most) of God's great blessings. The aging, the diminished, the unconventional of this world are seldom rated high on our "potential worth to me" scale. In our highly competitive, excellence-driven culture, they are often seen as inferior. They become disenfranchised and marginalized, relegated to programs or entities that will handle the "problem" for us, if indeed we are not able to eliminate them from our lives completely.

And so it was for me, at first. Accustomed to evaluating people from a worldly perspective, I missed the beauty, the potential, and the holy and precious aspects of my little daughter. Though I loved her passionately, I reacted only to her deficiency; I saw her differences as problems to be dealt with, behavior in need of "normalization." When we reject others, we fail to recognize that they have worthwhile lessons to teach and contributions to offer, and we diminish the beauty and potential of these rich opportunities. To change this pattern, we need to learn how to see from a different perspective. We need to retrain ourselves to evaluate our world and our lives from a different set of values. We need to develop the ability to see God, ourselves, and others from the perspective of God's heart.

> One of the teachers of religious law was standing there
> listening to . . . Jesus. . . . He asked, "Of all the com-
> mandments, which is the most important?" Jesus replied,
> "The most important commandment is this: 'Listen,
> O Israel! The LORD our God is the one and only LORD.
> And you must love the LORD your God with all your
> heart, all your soul, all your mind, and all your strength.'
> The second is equally important: 'Love your neighbor
> as yourself.' No other commandment is greater than
> these."[9]

SEEING GOD: LOVING FATHER

The first part of the passage that is known as the greatest command-ment is about the nature and person of God. To begin to see with God's heart, we must first acknowledge who He is—the one and only Lord. He isn't just any god, He isn't an option or choice—He is *the* God Almighty, *the* Creator of all things, *the* sovereign Ruler and Authority over everything! But He is also Abba—Papa—merciful, gentle, and *good* Father, who will go to all lengths to have an intimate relationship of trust, love, and total security with His beloved chil-dren. He is a Father who gives *only* good things to His children and never leaves them to fend for themselves during the hard times. Jesus told the people:

> You parents—if your children ask for a loaf of bread, do
> you give them a stone instead? Or if they ask for a fish,
> do you give them a snake? Of course not! So if you sinful

people know how to give good gifts to your children,
how much more will your heavenly Father give good
gifts to those who ask him.[10]

Although I believe that God has a sense of humor, God does *not*
play practical jokes on us. He showers us with His good things—but
often we don't recognize them because they unsettle our status quo or
they disrupt the plan we have made for our lives. To recognize that
everything that comes from God comes from and through His goodness requires us to look at things from an eternal perspective. That
can be done only through the "heart lens" of someone who is devoted
to knowing and loving God.

Jesus said that the ultimate good gift from the Father is the Holy
Spirit[11]—the breath of God in us. Through this Spirit in us, we are
able to begin to discern truth and beauty from God's perspective. It is
the Spirit of God in us, received when we put our trust in Christ, who
reveals to us the ways and things of God. And as we intentionally
acquiesce more and more of ourselves to the Spirit's leading and perspective, we will begin to experience the truth and beauty of God's
goodness in all things. The Bible assures us:

It was to us that God revealed these things by his Spirit.
For his Spirit searches out everything and shows us God's
deep secrets. . . . And we have received God's Spirit (not
the world's spirit), so we can know the wonderful things
God has freely given us.[12]

SEEING SELF: BELOVED CHILD OF GOD

Jesus told us that the greatest commandment—the greatest thing we
will ever do—is to love God with our whole hearts, souls, minds, and
strength. We will experience the greatest joy and peace when we
desire His relationship more than anything or anyone else in our lives;

when we seek after the knowledge, wisdom, and understanding of His ways as our highest priority; when we crave the good things He wants to give us more than any other distraction or pleasure; and when we choose to live the way He has shown us. As we begin to welcome His completely sufficient and yet totally unfathomable love for us, we find ourselves loving Him with more and more of our attention, attitudes, desires, and actions.

But the second part of that greatest commandment is to love others as ourselves. For those of us who have been scarred by the brutal nature of this world, loving ourselves can become self-protective and self-promotional. Before we can love others the way God desires us to love them, we must begin to see ourselves as God sees us—as His own beloved children.

When we begin to see with our own eyes and comprehend through our own experiences the trustworthy, unconditional, and never-disappointing love of our heavenly Father, we are then ready to look with fresh eyes at ourselves. When we base others' value on their worth to us, it is primarily because we see ourselves as vulnerable and weak.

As infants, we had no problem trusting. We giggled with ease and openly welcomed the hands that fed, bathed, and held us. We had no problem believing that we deserved to be loved and cared for, regardless of whether we were hungry or satisfied, clean or dirty, happy or fussy. We had no identity crisis from being completely dependent on others. We saw ourselves as objects of love and affection, and trusted confidently in the care of our parents. Of course, life and circumstances soon interrupted such security, and we all found ourselves pricked by the diaper pins of an impatient changing; feeling the brunt of an irritable, tired, and maybe even resentful caretaker; and fearing the loss of attention or provision—or even love—from those we relied on most. We no longer felt precious or protected, and as a result, we became self-protective and cautious. But when we begin to experience the love of an Abba—Papa—God who cares about our every need, who promises never to leave us, and who always keeps His promises, we begin to loosen our grip of self-preservation, self-centeredness, and self-focus. We allow ourselves to start feeling loved as adored children of God.

"Blessed is she who has believed that what the Lord has said to her will be accomplished!"[13]

SEEING OTHERS: BELOVED FAMILY MEMBERS

God loves each of us just because we exist—not because of what we have to offer or what we can do for Him. When we can begin to feel loved and cared for, no matter how slightly, by the almighty Creator of the universe, we inherit a new freedom to see others just as they are, totally separate from their potential to enhance or encumber our own lives. We begin to appreciate the immense value they have and the unique, exquisite blessings they are capable of bringing into our lives. They have an unexpected capacity for enhancing us in the most astonishing and wonder-filled ways.

This is not a romanticized sentiment. The perspective of God's heart is seldom the easy path! To see from God's heart means that many times our hearts must first be broken. Even the Holy Spirit is imparted to us as a result of the brokenness of Christ. God's blessing is often a path of immense sorrow, of letting go—letting go of *our* dreams and expectations so that we will be open to new possibilities. It is often a path of hard labor, relentless commitment, and unswerving devotion. Rarely is it a path of comfort or calm. But it is the key to joy that does not rely on circumstance, fulfillment that cannot be diminished, and peace that cannot even be explained![14]

Seeing others from God's heart is to see them for who they are—the precious, adored children of God, no matter their condition or circumstance. To love others as ourselves is to realize that we are all a part of God's plan and therefore a part of each other. We acknowledge that God has created us for the purpose and privilege of glorifying Him and being loved by Him. He has created every other person for that same reason. We share God's vision for each other, and we share God's intention for each other—to be loved and to love.

LOVE

In his Gospel, John called himself Christ's beloved, the one Jesus loved.[15] That indicates that John felt totally accepted by Christ. Yet a study of the Gospels quickly reveals that John was far from perfect. Jesus referred to him and James as "Sons of Thunder," and one time John asked Jesus if he could call down fire and ruination on a whole village because it had not welcomed Him![16] (It's slightly amusing to note that John makes no reference of this incident in his Gospel but leaves it to Luke to relate this undoubtedly embarrassing event.)

Christ's love is not judgmental. It does not keep score. It is one of acceptance. Christ recognizes the weakness and fallibility of people; He does not turn a blind eye to our mistakes and sinfulness. Yet instead of giving us labels, He offers us forgiveness. Instead of rejecting us, He gives us a chance to get better. Jesus explained to His disciple John that He had come to save people not to destroy them![17] When confronted by a woman who had committed adultery, Jesus challenged her accusers to examine their own lives before condemning her, and then He instructed her to go and make the necessary changes in her life.[18]

"Come to me," Christ urged the people, "all of you who are weary and carry heavy burdens, and I will give you rest."[19] And come they did! The sick, the oppressed, the poor, the outcasts, the very young, the very old . . . the fringes of society. They came, and they were welcomed. They were valued; they were seen and heard.

ACCEPTANCE

Love is about acceptance: accepting the value of another human being. Accepting his worth, but also accepting his weakness, his pain, his neediness. Accepting that she matters and that her life matters.

Love also involves accepting that some things cannot be changed and that those things do not diminish the significance of a soul. And love is about accepting the things that do change—the human condition that is constantly evolving, improving, or deteriorating. This kind of love encourages growth and healing. It results in joy and peace because it breaks down barriers. Acceptance changes our thinking from "me and you" to "we," from "us and them" to just "us."

The night before His death, Jesus' thoughts and prayers were that all Christians would come to fully accept and love one another. Christ prayed, "I pray that they will all be one, just as you [God the Father] and I are one."[20]

INCLUSION

When we begin to accept others, we gradually become others-focused. We empathize with people's fears and experiences of rejection, exclusion, and anonymity. We want to know more about them and to share their experiences, insights, and perspectives. Rather than avoiding them, we are moved to welcome them into our midst—cautiously at first, but eventually into our very lives. With time, our fear of their differences starts to diminish, and our reluctance to be burdened by them (or sometimes even associated with them) is slowly transformed to a recognition of their personhood—their true identities beyond their appearances or circumstances.

When we begin to see the hearts of others, we realize the common thread that exists, by the intention of our Creator, in all of us. It *is* possible for differences to become minimized as we attempt to appreciate the similarities we share with one another. Solomon said, "Nothing under the sun is truly new."[21] As we start to break down the barriers between us, we discover that we can share each other's burdens, encourage each other in our troubles, and celebrate each other on our journeys through life. God has given us each as a gift to and for one another.

RECEIVING

The ultimate expression of love is not just in giving; it is also in receiving. Love is when we affirm that *every* human being has something of essential value to give us—some precious attribute, quality, or nature that enhances, blesses, or beautifies our lives. Love involves receiving the eternal qualities we are each endowed with by the Spirit (love, joy, peace, patience, kindness, goodness, faithfulness, gentleness, and self-control) for the sole purpose of communicating God's glory to one another.[22] Love is when we intentionally seek and receive whatever is noble, whatever is right, whatever is pure, whatever is lovely, whatever is admirable—anything excellent or praiseworthy—from one another.[23]

Christ *received* the little children in His midst.[24] He took joy in those around Him. He communicated their value by showing that they had something that was worthy for Him to receive!

POSTSCRIPT

This community of love is not impossible, nor is it easy. As I write these words, I am sitting at the dining room table in one of the houses at the L'Arche Daybreak community near Toronto, a faith-based community for people with intellectual disabilities. I am moved by the dedication of workers and core members alike to the practice of living out Christ's mandate for us to love one another and live in peace with one another. Make no mistake, it takes commitment and absolute resolve, as well as willingness, action, discipline, and sometimes a dogged stick-to-itiveness, to persevere here. There is nothing sentimental or quaint about this place. It is filled with hard work and undignified practicality! But I have listened to the individuals' stories, triumphs, and failures, their accounts of overcoming as well as breaking down. I am struck by how consistently breaking points can become the very starting points of true healing, love, acceptance, inclusion, and receiving.

Labels, positions, and compartmentalization are minimized here. This is likely the most honest place outside of a delivery room that I have ever seen. Actually, in many ways it reminds me of a delivery room. When my granddaughter was born, I had the incredible privilege of being there, holding my daughter Michelle's hand. I was fully present for every pain, encouragement, and frustration as she delivered her firstborn. At the end of the hours of gruelingly unpretentious and painful labor, I witnessed the first breath of a new life. I heard the protesting yells from newly filled lungs, and I wept at the precious beauty born from pain. There is no more humbling or empowering experience in human nature than childbirth.

This community reminds me of that experience. I see the brutal reality and pain of broken lives, the glamourless caretaking and neediness represented here. But from this place, new lives—lives of worth and value and purpose—emerge, but not from programs, philosophies, or formulas. Instead, they come from brokenness that is accepted, included, and then empowered into a thing of value, beauty, and blessing, ready to be given to those who can recognize that there is something here to receive.

We *can* create a place in our hearts, our lives, our homes, our communities, even our world where:

> *The fringe become central,*
> *the rejected become essential,*
> *the unwelcome become included,*
> *beauty is reflected in brokenness,*
> *and forgiveness is inspired by flaw.*

Love is person, and love is a verb. It is not merely an emotion or a feeling. And for the Christian, it is not an option. It is the person of God, and it is the demonstration of His nature, through the Holy Spirit, in and by us.

QUESTIONS

Consider a time in your life when you felt rejected, excluded, or ridiculed because of some factor over which you had no control. What effect did that experience have on you? How did it change your perception of yourself or those who rejected you?

Think back to a time when you rejected, excluded, or ridiculed someone else because of some factor over which they had no control. Try to remember your motivation or attitude at the time.

Read and reflect on Matthew 25:31-46. At the end of this passage, Jesus said, "I tell you the truth, when you refused to help the least of these my brothers and sisters, you were refusing to help me." What emotions does this passage evoke in light of the previous question?

As believers, we look to Jesus as our source of blessing, comfort, guidance, and strength. How does that image fit with the idea of seeing Christ in the beggar, the stranger, the prisoner, the lonely, and the sick?

What does it mean to you to "see from God's heart"?

Mark 12:29-31 says, "The most important commandment is this: 'Listen, O Israel! The LORD our God is the one and only LORD. And you must love the LORD your God with all your heart, all your soul, all your mind, and all your strength.' The second is equally important: 'Love your neighbor as yourself.' No other command- ment is greater than these." Using this verse, prayerfully consider some practical ways you can begin to see God, yourself, and others from His heart-perspective.

5

Stay Where You Are

GROWING UP

Despite all these things, overwhelming victory
is ours through Christ, who loved us.
ROMANS 8:37

THE STRUGGLE

It's amazing what happens when we begin to pray that we will see things from God's perspective, that God will allow us to love freely without fear or judgment. It is even more amazing what happens to the recipient of that love. As I truly began to accept Nori the way she was, with no demands, no expectations—just because she was precious to God and to me—she began to bloom. She was like a little rosebud that had been tightly closed against the pain and hurt of this world. The more love she received without condition or expectation, the safer she began to feel and the more she began, gradually and cautiously, to open up.

It started when Michelle and Joshua and I would spend time every day lying next to her, wiggling our fingers in front our faces. We called it our "finger game time." I began to regiment our day; we kept a strict and unshakable schedule. My thinking was that if Nori knew what to expect, she would become more secure in her surroundings. After every event that involved touching—feeding, bathing, changing—I would allow her a time in bed to be left alone. Slowly she started to stay awake during these activities, still wiggling her fingers in front of her eyes, of course, but awake! She also began to stop concentrating on her hands briefly and allowed us to get closer and closer to her on the floor during our finger game time. And then one morning, a miracle! I went to get her up to start our day, and she made eye contact. Just briefly, but it was there. A connection!

Nori's progress was swift and wonderful. Every day she seemed to open up just a little bit more—and then one day, noise! She cried, and it was the first time she had made sound. When I put her in the bath, instead of falling asleep or "going into her hands," as we called it, she cried! So did I. Bath time had been a particularly structured time. Even though she had always slept through it, I would gently wash her with my hands, softly speaking to her, telling her what was happening, assuring her that we loved her, and quietly singing my favorite songs to her. Then I would dry her and put lotion on her the same way. Today was no different, except that instead of sleeping through it, she cried. A few days later, at the end of bath time, when I dried her off, she stopped crying. She put her little head on my shoulder and allowed me to caress and hold her without falling into sleep.

Over the next few weeks, she became a human love sponge. Every day was a new beginning; she began to open up to us—slowly, yes, but consistently. She spent more and more time awake and less and less time "into her hands." She began making eye contact with others and making regular baby noises; she even started rolling over. Our pediatrician was not as enthusiastic as we were. No matter what progress I reported to him, he was quick to point out what milestones she *hadn't* reached.

The one supportive doctor we had was our plastic surgeon. He told us not to worry, that God had this little one in His hands. We had decided to let everyone adjust to her arrival before going ahead with surgery, so it was close to four months after she came that we began to prepare for Nori's first operation to close her cleft lip. Because of the severity of her bilateral cleft as well as further damage that had been done by her environment in Korea, we were warned that it would be a particularly difficult repair.

The day of the operation arrived. We had already been through five surgeries between Michelle and Joshua, so we felt pretty savvy about the whole hospital routine. The surgery took more than twice as long as predicted, but at last our surgeon appeared. The operation had indeed been difficult, the most difficult of his career, in fact. He told us that at one point he almost despaired of completely closing her cleft, but he felt certain that the results were going to be good. Since she had been anesthetized for so long, it took her hours to wake up, and when she did it was late in the day. Greg and I stayed with her late into the night but then decided to go home for a while to rest and spend some time with the other two children. That turned out to be a dreadful mistake; we never should have left her alone. When I returned the next morning, I discovered that the night nurses had decided that an MR (their code for *mentally retarded*) patient didn't need all the toys we had put in her bed, so they distributed them around the room to the other patients. We had carefully chosen Nori's favorite toys from home to help her feel as safe and secure as possible. The nurses also had not bothered to clean her sutures or change her diaper all night. By the time I arrived, Nori had completely regressed back to her original behavior. It was hard to tell who was more furious, our surgeon or me! Nori was given a private room; the nurses were given a tongue-lashing. But the damage had been done. I was devastated.

I picked up my beautiful baby and began to rock her. In His amazing grace, the presence of God surrounded us, and I realized that it was okay. We had seen a different side of Nori for a time, but if she needed to return to where she was before, even if she needed to stay there, it was okay. *She* was okay. Our love for her didn't depend on her behavior or progress; we just loved *her*. Not what she was or could be—just her, herself, because she was precious.

In that hospital at the time, young children were not allowed to visit the patients. But a few days later, Greg decided to smuggle Michelle and Joshua up to Nori's room. She was lying in her bed, once again wiggling her fingers in front of her face, when the kids came bounding in. They were both excited to see their baby sister, and each had a toy for her. At the sound of their voices, Nori put down her hands, turned her head toward the sound—then squealed with excitement and "came back" to us! That was the last time Nori ever went to that "secret place" within herself. Not even many future surgeries, illnesses, and injuries drew her there again. From that moment on it seemed as if she could not progress fast enough. Every day brought something new! Nori's life verse surely has been Philippians 3:13-14: "I focus on this one thing: Forgetting the past and looking forward to what lies ahead, I press on to reach the end of the race and receive the heavenly prize for which God, through Christ Jesus, is calling us."

Nori's last physical hurdle was her legs. Even as tiny as she was, during the last few months she had been in Korea she had apparently outgrown the bed she lived in. Her legs had been forced into a "frog leg" position, and the muscles had atrophied and degenerated. We were told that she probably would never walk. She had begun scooting—not really crawling; she couldn't get up on her knees. But she was curious and adventuresome, and nothing could stop her from getting where she wanted to go. When she was twenty-one months old, we prepared to celebrate her first Christmas with us. The afternoon of Christmas Eve, we stopped at an open house given by some close friends from our church. The men were in the family room, the women in the kitchen. Nori was at the far end of the kitchen, playing on the floor with some pots and pans, when she heard me laugh. She looked up at me and smiled. Then, without hesitation, she pulled herself up to her feet and toddled across the floor with her arms opened wide for me to pick her up. None of us could believe what we were seeing. It was our own Christmas miracle!

Nori needed a lot of therapy in the years to come—physical therapy, occupational therapy, speech therapy—but each step came with enthusiasm and excitement. She became a carrier of joy and love wherever she went. Her ability to embrace life was and still is an inspiration to everyone, and especially to me.

God's blessings are so awesome! We become a part of God's *better* plan when we first believe in His goodness, let go of our agendas, embrace the reality of here and now in our lives, and endeavor to see the gifts that God gives us from His heart's perspective. But His blessings also require *staying*—the Bible calls it *perseverance*.

Over the next three years we adopted three more children from Korea: two-year-old Nicholas, three-year-old Christopher, and fourteen-year-old Suzanne. They all came with "special need" and they all came in their own unique manner, with their own particular challenges.

As our family grew, Joshua's behavior grew more and more erratic. His antics became more dangerous, his moods more extreme. He had a brilliant mind, yet he failed continually at school. He challenged every authority in his life; every system, every rule, every standard was like a personal fight for survival. Unknown to us, by sixth grade Josh was drinking alcohol on the playground at school, seeing how intoxicated he could get without anyone noticing. By junior high he was doing drugs. We were absolutely clueless! We were a family who talked about drugs at the dinner table and read God's Word with our dessert every night. We were actively involved in our children's lives, in their schools and activities, and in our church. Our family was our priority. We appeared to be the textbook example of "Christian" parenting! I was even a frequent speaker on godly parenting at parent functions. I realize now that the enemy can infiltrate any home. As parents we must realize that our children have been given the same free will that God has given us. When they make wrong choices, parents need to unashamedly seek support, prayer, and sometimes even professional help. Adam and Eve had the perfect parent (God the Father) and perfect conditions (Eden), yet they still made devastating choices: listening to Satan and following his tempting.

The more outlandish Joshua's behavior, the more desperate we became. He was arrested for shoplifting and sentenced to court-ordered counseling—another challenge for him to manipulate. The counselor had no clue about his drug use and was convinced that Josh was a bright kid who fell in with the wrong crowd. Of course, I believed him. I later came to realize that "bright" kids don't hang out with the wrong crowd.

Joshua was self-destructing. Over the next two years we enrolled him in three different high schools, until one day everything fell apart. With growing tensions at home, Josh finally snapped. Unknown to us, Josh was falling into a dark world of depression, drug and alcohol abuse, and role-playing Internet games. When we discovered him at 2 a.m. hiding under the kitchen table, secretly playing the game, we knew we were all in over our heads. He admitted that he was out of control and needed help. We promised we would get help the next morning and assured him not to worry. Later, when I dropped him off at school, I reassured him and told him that everything would be okay. I watched him walk toward the school and then turned and drove home. But Josh never made it to class. He had stolen my credit card, hopped on the next bus, and ended up in Texas, with people he had "met" on the Internet helping him along the way. It was weeks before we tracked him down, and years before he conquered his demons.

Josh descended into a hellish existence of drugs, depression, and self-destructive behavior. He was hospitalized several times and spent a year in a locked residential care center. He overdosed accidentally and intentionally. And once more in my life I raged against God. God was *not* good. God was *not* fair. God was *not* just. Joshua had been *born* addicted. It was not his choice! God could have prevented this if He had wanted to. Josh had been an innocent victim at birth. How was that fair? How was that kind? How was that loving?

The Old Testament includes a story about Jacob, who one night found himself alone on the banks of the Jabbok River as he was preparing to be reunited with his estranged brother, Esau. Scripture tells us that a "man" came and wrestled with Jacob all night. At dawn, the man struck Jacob's hip and knocked it out of socket. Then the man said,

> "Let me go, for the dawn is breaking!"
>
> But Jacob said, "I will not let you go unless you bless me."
>
> "What is your name?" the man asked.
>
> He replied, "Jacob."
>
> "Your name will no longer be Jacob," the man told him. "From now on you will be called Israel, because you have fought with God and with men and have won."
>
> "Please tell me your name," Jacob said.
>
> "Why do you want to know my name?" the man replied. Then he blessed Jacob there.
>
> Jacob named the place Peniel (which means "face of God"), for he said, "I have seen God face to face, yet my life has been spared."[1]

The Bible tells us that Jacob was indeed struggling with the Lord Himself that night, as is attested by the name given to that place. Well, I didn't meet the Lord on the banks of the river Jabbok. I met him in my kitchen, at 2 a.m., and there we struggled till dawn. My rage at God's unfairness to our son was intense. And God let me rage all night long. I was angry and scared and bitter, and He let me vent with full force until

I had worn myself out. I would not let go until God gave me an answer! And there, in the still, quiet loneliness of my kitchen, just as the first rays of dawn were beginning to shine, God touched my soul. I felt as well as heard God's love for my son. **I love him more than you do. Joshua is first and foremost My son, and I love him.**

In my mind, I was suddenly given a picture of Joshua as he had been at about two years old: healthy, happy, running with his arms open toward his father. Except this time, he was running toward his heavenly Father. God did not give me a reassurance that things would ever be okay or that Josh would ever be healthy, sober, or happy again. But He did tell me that He loved Josh, that He cared more about him than I did, and that He would never leave him. And I believed Him. *Blessed is she who has believed that what the Lord has said to her will be accomplished!* In Scripture, a person's name says as much about his character as it does about his identity. Like Jacob, I had my name changed by God that night—from *despair* to *hope*.

STAYING WHERE YOU ARE

The apostle Paul learned from his own experiences about the process of moving from despair to hope. He wrote that we can rejoice in our sufferings because we know that suffering produces perseverance, and perseverance produces the character that gives birth to *hope*. And that "hope does not disappoint us, because God has poured out his love into our hearts by the Holy Spirit, whom he has given us."[2]

The gift of joy that is found in suffering is not suffering for its own sake. Rather, it's the opportunity that suffering brings for us to rely completely on God long enough to experience His power, His provision, and His presence in character-changing ways. That experiential knowledge of God's faithfulness is what produces hope that will not disappoint, because it is hope we have counted on and hope that has

not let us down. It is hope based on the love God has poured out on us
as we depend upon Him.

There comes a time when all we can do is to hold on and believe
what God has told us. It is a time of *staying*.

- Staying *obedient*, regardless of the circumstances around us. We
  continue to do the things we need to do.
- Staying *faithful*, regardless of our feelings. We choose to believe
  that all things are possible[3] and that even if we never
  see the fulfillment of God's promises in this life, He is true
  to His promises and He will do what He says He will do!
- Staying *where we are*, even when we want to escape, deny, or
  withdraw. We depend for a season on the body of believers we
  are a part of, allowing them to give us support and encouragement (and an occasional meal!).
- Staying *in an attitude of love*, even when we hate the situation
- or condition we find ourselves in. We intentionally resolve
  that love never gives up, love will never lose faith, love will
  always stay hopeful, and love will endure through every
  circumstance.[4]

The apostle Paul wrote,

> Can anything ever separate us from Christ's love? Does it
> mean he no longer loves us if we have trouble or calam-
> ity, or are persecuted, or hungry, or destitute, or in dan-
> ger, or threatened with death? . . . No, despite all these
> things, overwhelming victory is ours through Christ,
> who loved us.[5]

Victory will come only if we hold on and stay in Christ, in faith,
in trust.

PERSEVERANCE

Perseverance is not a common concept these days. The word itself evokes negative, queasy feelings. Think of other words associated with perseverance: *commitment, endurance, hardship*. One hardly speaks of persevering through the good times! Even Scripture seems to hold out a reward in heaven as the only motivation for perseverance. And although we know that heavenly gain is the best and longest-lasting a reward (it's eternal, after all!), that is often cold comfort while we are struggling to hold on in this life. But the fact is, perseverance properly experienced is its own reward! It is precisely this steadfast devotion to seeing things through, to finishing well the task put before us[6] that draws us into an intimacy with God that we never could have experienced otherwise.

PRAYER

What helps us persevere? How do we hold on until we get to the blessing? The single most important support is prayer. Prayer is our communication with God; it is our lifeline, our connection to the Creator! But prayer is often misunderstood, poorly practiced, or avoided completely. Prayer is often a mystery. We ask questions such as: Why must we pray? Doesn't God already know what's going on? Doesn't He know what I need and want? For prayer to be our lifeline in times of trouble, we need to grow in our understanding and experience of what prayer is, what prayer does, and why prayer connects us with God.

Many of us have been taught that prayer is a formal litany of prepared statements to a distant God. Or we have become accustomed to praying our "shopping list" of requests and problems, as well as *our* solutions for those problems: "Lord, please do this for me. Solve my problems this way. Make my husband (son, daughter, mother, boss, teacher, coworker) do this instead of that!" Then, as an afterthought or possible loophole, we may throw in, "But Thy will be done!" Petition is certainly a type of prayer, but that is not communing with

God. Communication is a two-way process in which both parties converse. And it has been my experience that what God has to say is infinitely more significant, useful, and yes, divine, than anything we might have to say. Yet the amazing thing is, He *wants* to listen to us! He encourages us to bring everything to Him—not just our needs and desires, but more important, our feelings, our fears, our thoughts, our hearts. God desires two-way communication with us, heart to heart! That is communion—a spiritual joining together of two hearts.

STILLNESS

How do we practice such communion with God? It requires time and quiet. Not just physical quiet—though that is important—but emotional, intellectual, and spiritual stillness. For most of us, just being quiet for ten minutes is nearly impossible. We are accustomed to noise—and we will create our own, if necessary. We walk into a room and turn on the television, radio, or stereo. If that isn't possible, we find ourselves humming or whistling or even talking to ourselves. Our culture has become uncomfortable with quiet, and trying to calm and quiet our minds is an even harder endeavor. We are busy and task driven; if our bodies aren't doing something, our minds must be.

But the first step to communing with God is stillness. And that takes time and, paradoxically, commitment and effort. We must make it a priority to schedule some time—free from appointments, free from interruptions, free from any other schedule or agenda—for the mere purpose of just *being* with God. It is important to take steps to quiet our environment or to find a quiet place. Then we can begin to calm our souls—to set aside our thoughts and worries and focus our whole attention on being fully present with God. We must also set aside any goals we may have for this time and allow God to set the agenda. This is not a task or an exercise or something we are doing. It is an opportunity to rest in God's presence and let Him lead the way. Stillness is not about doing something; it is about *being somewhere*—

being in the quiet presence of God. It is not about producing some-thing; it is about *becoming something*—becoming intimate with God. The psalms tell us to "be still before the LORD and wait patiently" and to "know that I am God."[7]

When we are in the midst of crisis or hardship, we can find it diffi-cult to calm down and be still. Most of us either go into frantic-prob-lem-solving-I-must-be-*doing*-something mode, or we withdraw into private, lonely isolation. God wants to meet us in both of these places. He wants to console, strengthen, and assure us, but often we miss the provision He is trying to give, not because He is not offering it or because He has some preset procedure we must follow before He will give it to us, but because we are too busy to stop and receive it. At other times we become so focused on our own pain that we withdraw and do not hear Him or see Him reaching out to us, offering us Him-self as our comfort, power, and relief for this journey. "The LORD longs to be gracious to you; he rises to show you compassion. For the LORD is a God of justice. Blessed are all who wait for him!"[8]

SCRIPTURE

One of the most effective aids in quieting our minds is Scripture, which refocuses our thoughts from the pressures, problems, and demands of our lives to the person and presence of God. It also allows us a foundation to test what we perceive during this quiet time. Does it come from God or from my own thoughts? If it comes from God, it will *never* contradict what He has revealed about Himself, His will, or His ways through His Word.

If it has been our habit to spend time in God's Word on a regular basis, we can draw on certain passages that hold special meaning and insight for us. But often in times of turmoil, we need a fresh word or direction. The psalms are always a good place to start. The psalms, filled with honest and passionate emotion, are the hymnal and prayer book of the Bible. We find ourselves pouring out our hearts through the psalmists' words, and we can begin to envision the person of God in the descriptive passages of God's beauty and power.

Another place to turn is the pages of the Gospels: Matthew, Mark, Luke, and John. These books reveal the heart and compassion of God through the life of Christ. Don't just read the words; try to hear them. As we spend time listening to His Word, we find ourselves being drawn closer to Him, wanting to spend time with Him. What makes the Bible more than just a "religious" book is that God Himself uses His Word to personally touch our lives—it is what the writer of Hebrews meant when he said that God's Word is "living and active."[9]

JOURNAL

I can't overstate the value of keeping a journal through difficult times. God uses our honest outpouring of emotion to reveal Himself to us and to comfort us in our pain and to bring healing. When Moses was confronted by God at the burning bush, he asked God who He was. God told Moses that He is "I AM."[10] God tells us the same thing. When we honestly show God what we are feeling and thinking, He replies by telling us who He is. Every time God says "I AM" (sometimes translated as *Yahweh*), He is telling us who He is in us, in our pain, and in our circumstances. He tells us what He will do in our lives when He tells us who He is.

It's kind of like a twelve-step meeting. I introduce myself to God by saying who I am, and then God answers by telling me who He wants to be in my life! (To see some other names of God, review appendix A on page 147.)

Me: Hello, God. I am scared today.
God: **Welcome, I am your strength for today.**[11]
Me: God, I am so alone tonight.

God: **Come to me; I am with you.**[12]
Me: Lord, I am in darkness and uncertainty.
God: **See me; I am the Light.**[13]
Me: Lord! I am in such need!
God: **I am your provider.**[14]

Writing down our thoughts and feelings in simple, honest words helps us clarify them, and writing down God's responses to us helps us grasp what He is really saying, revealing, or inspiring in us. When God speaks to us, it is worth remembering! We are given an example of this in the Old Testament book of Habakkuk:

> I will climb up to my watchtower and stand at my
> guardpost. There I will wait to see what the LORD says
> and how he will answer my complaint. Then the LORD
> said to me, "Write my answer plainly on tablets. . . . If it
> seems slow in coming, wait patiently, for it will surely
> take place."[15]

God is waiting for us to get still, hear Him, and invite Him into our current situations. Jesus calls to us, "Here I am! I stand at the door and knock. If anyone hears my voice and opens the door, I will come in and eat with him, and he with me."[16]

COMMUNITY

To persevere means to *stay*: to stay in prayer, to stay in the stillness of God's presence, to stay in the truth of God's Word, to stay in communion with God. It is also crucial that we stay in community. Community can mean many different things, but a scriptural image is being part of a body of believers. Traditionally that denotes a church or congregation, but the term doesn't mean that exclusively. When we become Christians, God grafts us into the existing body of all believers. With all other Christians, we share a common allegiance to God the Creator, a common belief in the sufficiency of Christ's sacrifice to reconcile our broken relationship with God and assure us eternal salvation, a common destiny heavenward, and a common calling—to love and glorify God.[17]

But it is also important that we belong to a community of individuals who encourage our beliefs and callings by regularly coming together to worship, pray, study God's Word, and support and help one another. The early believers called this community a church. In the book of Acts, the early church was defined by their practice of community and fellowship. "They worshiped together at the Temple each day, met in homes for the Lord's Supper, and shared their meals with great joy and generosity—all the while praising God and enjoying the goodwill of all the people."[18] Throughout the New Testament, we see examples of such groups meeting in homes for the purpose of supporting each member's faith as well as helping to encourage each other in whatever they might be going through—good times or hard times.[19]

The Bible tells a wonderful story about some companions of a paralyzed man who took their friend to Jesus to be healed. Not being able to push through the crowd, the men hauled their friend, stretcher and all, up to the roof of the house where the Lord was staying. They broke through the ceiling and lowered the man right in front of where Jesus was standing! According to both Mark's and Luke's accounts of the story, when Jesus saw the faith of the companions, He was moved to respond to the man's needs.[20]

Sometimes in our deepest times of crisis or grief or stress or just fatigue, it seems that we are not able to pray for ourselves. Sometimes we even purposely avoid God out of anger, fear, or weariness. As the psalmist cried out, "I am worn out from sobbing."[21] It is in those times that we must rely on the prayers and support of our faith community. And though it is often tempting to shut out the people around us in our times of need, it is precisely those times when we must allow ourselves to be ministered to, in prayer and in deeds. The Bible is filled with "one anothers"—things that God has placed us in the body to do for and accept from each other. When we are struggling, it is extremely difficult to humble ourselves and ask for help, yet that is the very reason God has put us in community! Every ability God has given us is not for our own edification but to glorify and serve Him by helping one another. And when it is our time to accept help, we must receive from the people whom God has purposely placed in our lives for that very reason.

One last word about community: The time to find or develop our community is not when crisis comes. It takes time to develop trust and to discover our gifts and abilities in the context of giving to and receiving from one another. Scripture shows us that from the time Adam discovered his need for a companion, God has created us to be communal.[22] We cannot become all that God has planned us to be on our own. Each one of us plays an important role in the well-being of the whole body, and the whole body is important for the well- being of each part.[23] (My hand cannot reach its potential without the arm, and my arm cannot reach its full potential apart from the hand.) I do not believe that it is possible to discover God's better plan for our lives on our own. Although times of solitude are crucial for spiritual growth, we are created and called to be in relationships within the context of the body of Christ—both universal and local.

When trials hit, we must stay where we are. We must hold on until the blessing comes. As we persevere through our circumstances, we can draw nearer to God through the disciplines of prayer, stillness, Bible reading, journaling, and community. (For more information on these topics and some material to get you started, review the Prayer and Solitude Guides in appendix B.)

QUESTIONS

We all go through some difficult times in our lives. If you are in a place of calm right now, consider how spiritually prepared you are for the difficult times you may face in the future. Consider your prayer life, your familiarity with God's Word, and your involvement in the body of Christ. What steps do you need to take to begin or continue to grow in these areas?

If you are currently facing a critical time, what steps do you need to take to help you persevere?

Spend some time thinking back over past times of trouble or hardship that you have gone through. What were some of your most imperative needs during those days? Were you able to reach out to God? How did God meet your needs (or meet you) during those times?

God reveals who He is by the names and descriptions He gives for Himself throughout Scripture. (Appendix A, starting on page 147, includes many of these names.) Prayerfully consider which of His names are the most meaningful to you. Why? What "I AM" do you need God to be in your life right now?

Over and over in Scripture, God tells us to call on His name. Spend some time in prayer calling on the name that you need Him to be for you.

Consider scheduling a time to get away to a quiet place so you can just be still and wait for God. (See appendix B for several prayer guides that can assist you in getting started.)

6

Expect to Be Blessed

THE FULFILLMENT

&

"For I know the plans I have for you," says the LORD. "They are plans
for good and not for disaster, to give you a future and a hope. In those
days when you pray, I will listen. If you look for me wholeheartedly, you will
find me. I will be found by you," says the LORD.
JEREMIAH 29:11–14

GREAT EXPECTATIONS

I once heard a speaker talk about his "life verse," Jeremiah 29:11 (see
above). That sounded like a pretty good promise to me. Frankly, since
at that point in time, God's plans didn't look all that great—at least
where they concerned Joshua—I thought maybe I should look into it.

The problem with claiming that verse is that we often don't bother
to look at the twenty-eight chapters of Jeremiah that precede chapter
29. (Basic Bible study skill #1: Whenever you come upon a "but," "for,"
"wherefore," or "therefore," you need to ask, "What is it there *for?*")

The truth is that the chapters leading up to 29:11 are pretty grim.
God is telling the prophet Jeremiah that Israel was going to be disci-
plined and tested because of their generations of sin, that things
were going to get very hard for them, and that they were going to
feel as if God had turned against them and abandoned them. The

speaker hadn't looked at Jeremiah 29:10: "You will be in Babylon for seventy years." God was telling Israel that the powerful kingdom of Babylon was going to conquer them and that they were going to be held in captivity for seventy years! Only then came the turning point, the all-important "but":

> "*But* then I will come and do for you all the good things I
> have promised, and I will bring you home again. For I
> know the plans I have for you," says the LORD. "They are
> plans for good and not for disaster, to give you a future
> and a hope."[1]

Strangely, the verse brings me *more* assurance when put in context. God hasn't promised us easy lives with no problems. In fact, God uses the consequences of our choices and the circumstances of our lives to bring us back to Him and His ways. But He tells us to trust Him and believe that His plans are good!

The next verses are even more important. God tells His prophet that when the people were in Babylon—which for the ancient Israelites was a literal city of captivity but for us symbolizes any time of suffering or feeling abandoned and powerless—if in those times we will turn and look for Him in earnest, He will be found! Now there's a promise we can cling to.

> In those days when you pray, I will listen. If you look for
> me wholeheartedly, you will find me.

By the mid-1990s, our children were all approaching their late teens and adulthood—some with more grace than others. Joshua, not quite eighteen, was on a runaway train headed for disaster. After completing a year of intense psychological and drug treatment at a residential facility in Utah, he came home in worse condition than ever.

However, he was still alive! He once asked me if I knew why he was always doing dangerous things—even as a little boy. Why had he always picked the tallest trees to climb and then jump from? Because, he revealed to me, deep down inside, he knew that he would die by his own hand before his eighteenth birthday. But God had other plans for Joshua. Remember, his name means "God saves"!

Every day brought new hope and new fear. What were God's plans for this young man—so full of brilliance, talent, and sensitivity, yet so vexed by the demons of addiction and mental conflict? There was never any doubt that God *did* have a plan for Joshua. Even he had to admit that! Upon regaining consciousness after a particularly close suicide attempt, his first angry words were, "Why does God keep saving me?"

A turning point seemed to come in February, a few months before Josh turned nineteen. An accidental overdose at a party scared him; this time he didn't want to die. He was taken to the hospital and checked into a detox center. It took a week for him to get cleaned out, and then he voluntarily transferred to a hospital designed specifically for his type of problems. It was a rough year, but by October he was committed to living sober. With the help of daily recovery meetings and the recognition of his need for God's presence and power in his life, Josh struggled to reconcile with his past, rehabilitate his present, and even plan for a future . . . a future of good, not disaster, a future of hope.

Our lives took another turn. Josh became a regular at the local twelve-step recovery meetings. He also spoke to teenagers at rehab centers and began bringing other kids home with him. Boys and girls who had left or been kicked out of their own homes came to live with us for a while until they could get on their feet again. I was becoming a "mom" to even more kids! We had only a few rules: no "using" (drugs and alcohol were strictly off limits), no sex, come to church with us, and we don't want to hear about your past—our home is a "do over," and you start with a fresh reputation. (It sounds more philanthropic than it was. Frankly, I was afraid of what I might learn about the lives some of these kids had led. Sometimes it is better not to know.)

Time steadily advances; days, weeks, years pass. The crises of the moment do resolve, and by God's grace we learn, grow, and continue. If we have based our lives on the foundational fact of God's goodness, if we have attempted to loosen our grips on our own agendas and have endeavored—no matter how imperfectly—to face reality through God's perspective, then our perseverance does give way to maturity. The plans of God begin to grow clearer—in our outlooks as well as in our experiences.

God kept bringing Philippians 1:6 into my life. Our church sang it, my Bible seemed to open to it automatically, every radio preacher seemed to be teaching it. Over and over I kept "running into it," until finally I decided to pay attention.

> I am certain that God, who began the good work within
> you, will continue his work until it is finally finished on
> the day when Christ Jesus returns.

On a weekend of solitude, away by myself in a little cabin in the mountains of Big Bear, California, I spent three days meditating on this verse alone. I realized that it was a foundational truth that must be grasped if I was ever going to see beyond the moment and understand that the intricacies of today's experiences have meaning beyond the immediate. They are intended to fit together into a grander scheme— a heavenly, eternal patchwork. The way we grow through the daily events of our lives molds us into the vessels that God uses for His greater purposes.

During the dark times of Joshua's addictions, our daughter Nori introduced me to the writings of Henri Nouwen, a noted Harvard theologian who gave up the world of academia and dedicated his life to working and writing at the L'Arche Daybreak community for people with intellectual disabilities. Nouwen's inspirational and personal devotions on spiritual living and the pathway of Christian disciplines gave me insight and yearning for a deeper spiritual experience. Though I never had an opportunity to meet him, Nouwen became, in a very real way, my spiritual mentor. His books led me to a deeper understanding of God's heart as revealed through Scripture, prayer, and solitude. His honest vulnerability and passion offered me a companion in my despair and a confidant in my moments of struggle.

It was Nouwen I turned to when Josh faced his next crisis. As Josh struggled to maintain sobriety, he also struggled with his faith. As parents, Greg and I had always put a high priority on sharing our faith with our kids and exemplifying it to them. Greg's steady, solid, unwavering trust in God in all circumstances was a foundation for our family in general and an anchor for me in my times of struggle. Perhaps it was due to my desperate resolve that all my children accept Christ as Lord. (I often forgot that I was *only* their mother, not the Holy Spirit, and that it is by the Spirit that we are called and convinced of Christ's lordship.[2]) Or maybe it was my insistence that they believe the Bible (as if we can insist on another person believing something). But Josh wavered between belief and unbelief. He wasn't ready to accept someone else's faith as his own. He had seen so much in his young life—so much pain, suffering, ugliness, and despair—and he needed to find God for himself.

It was ironic that it took me so long to realize this about my son, because I also struggled with my faith in my youth. Raised in a Christian home, with a missionary-trained mother, I grew up believing in Christ and the Bible; yet during my college years, I turned away from my faith—only to later reclaim it for myself. I have always considered those years of "seeking" as a gift—a blessing—because they allowed me to discover my own need for, and relationship with, Christ. My faith became my own—not my mother's, not my church's, but my own. Yet somehow I had forgotten how necessary it was for my children to discover and develop their faith for themselves.

When Josh faced the double heartbreak of the death of a friend and the end of a serious relationship in the spring of 2001, it caused him to seriously question what he believed about God and about himself as a child of God. It also caused me to fear that he might return to drugs or alcohol or worse. In my fear, I gave him the book *Letters to Marc about Jesus*, by Henri Nouwen.[3] I wish I could say that I chose it because of its applicability to his problems, but the truth is, I had never read it. I picked it because Marc is Joshua's middle name! However, Josh did read the book and was deeply affected by it. Nouwen's words touched his heart and soul. And being Josh, he decided that he needed to get in touch with the author and talk to him in person. Not realizing that Nouwen had died several years earlier, Josh attempted to write to the author at the L'Arche Daybreak community in Toronto.[4] One of the longtime members of the community wrote back to Josh, explaining that Henri had died in September 1996. But God had plans for Joshua's future, and over the next few months they developed a relationship through e-mail. In August 2001, Josh was invited to come and visit Daybreak. At the end of his visit, Josh was invited to join the community as an assistant, and in January 2002, he moved to Toronto.

"He who began a good work in you will carry it on to completion."[5]

All the pain and brokenness that Joshua had experienced in his life was *exactly* what had prepared and molded him for working with broken people! In one of his early letters home, Josh wrote, "I know why I feel so at home and so comfortable here among the members of L'Arche. They are broken on the outside in the same way that I have been broken on the inside. Together, we become whole."

This last fall, as I sat in the Daybreak chapel at my son's wedding, surrounded by the people of this community who had made such an impact on the heart and work of Henri Nouwen, who in turn had made such an impact on my son and me, I was overwhelmed by the abundance of God's goodness and the brilliant details of His plan. God had brought Joshua to this place to bring purpose and meaning from his pain and brokenness. He had brought Josh into this community to transform his weakness into compassion, his struggle into service. And God had even provided this community as the place for Josh to meet and marry his beautiful, gentle bride, Meghan. The only thought that filled my mind and my heart was, "My cup overflows with blessings!"[6] Who would have thought it would work out this way? Only God! It was His *better* plan all along.

EXPECTING TO BE BLESSED

I have learned to *expect to be blessed*—on a daily basis. I have learned that God never wastes a hurt, never crushes a dream, and never leaves His work unfinished! God is in the business of changing things—changing pain into triumph, dreams into realities, and ordinary lives into blessings. But if we do not *expect* the blessing, we just might miss it. It is God's plan and delight to bless us, but we must remain on the course He has set for us long enough to get to the blessing, to have our lives and circumstances changed into a work of God. We must expect to be surprised by the results because things probably won't end up looking the way we had assumed—or sometimes even hoped—they would. But they *will* be better, whether we recognize it or not.

LOOKING FORWARD TO BLESSING: ENTITLEMENT VERSUS EXPECTATION

There is a diametric difference between expecting to be blessed because it is God's nature and desire to bless His children and expecting to be blessed because we believe that we somehow deserve it. God blesses us because it is His pleasure to do so, not because we in any way warrant it or are worthy of it. That is called *grace*—God's unmerited, undeserved, and unearned favor.

The "doctrine of entitlement" seems to be a popular trend these days. Essentially it goes like this: *If* I follow some simple three-step plan (or five steps or an acrostic), *then* God will bless me in some specifically prescribed method. That may be the formula for a good self-help plan, but it is certainly not the path to blessing! God does not bless us because He is obligated to reward our efforts. We do not and cannot earn or manipulate blessing. God does not respond to "I'll do this if You do that" sort of bargaining. He does not barter or trade. Paul tells us in Romans 9 that God's mercy is based on His choice, not our works, and that He chooses according to His own plan.[7]

Being blessed by the sovereign Creator of the universe is an overwhelmingly awesome experience, and *expecting* to be blessed by the sovereign Creator of the universe is a humble expectation. We must first realize our utter unworthiness to receive His notice, and then we must recognize our absolute ineptness to initiate such attention. Blessing is born of God's goodness alone. But if we do not train ourselves to look forward to the wonders and marvels God is going to do today, then we will most likely miss seeing them. We become consumed with our schedules, our agendas, our constantly moving and demanding lives. We become distracted by the pleasures or problems around us. We become discouraged by the seemingly uncontrollable events of our community, society, and world. The things we need to do, the things that entice or distract us, the things that frustrate and demean us, all rob our attention, and we forget to anticipate and notice what God is doing!

God is constantly doing. It is our joy and pleasure, as well as our privilege and responsibility, to recognize the evidence of His handiwork. Jesus told the people, "My Father is always working, and so am I."[8]

If we want to be blessed by the work that God is doing around and in us, we need to make an attitude adjustment. We need to develop a daily outlook of expectation! Expect Him to be working in our lives (blessing), and then pay attention to find out what He's doing and where He's doing it.

LOOKING FOR BLESSING: LIVING THE LIFE GOD BLESSES

How do we know where to look for evidence of God's work? God works where His will is being done. God works where His name is being called on. God works where His people are actively serving and working *in His name*. A lot of abuse has been given to the concept of "in His name." A false teaching asserts that *anything* we ask for using the name of Jesus in our request is instantly ours to claim. That simply isn't true. It doesn't matter how often I declare, "In the name of Jesus, I can fly"—it just isn't going to happen! It has nothing to do with my faith or lack thereof; it has everything to do with the fact that it isn't, never has been, and never will be God's plan that I be an airplane. When Paul claimed that he could do "all things through Him [Jesus Christ] who strengthens me," he was referring to victorious living in all circumstances, not boasting about his own achievements.[9]

To ask, to work, to serve in *the name of Jesus* means to do so in the very same nature, attitude, motivation, and example that was Christ's. When Christ said, "Follow me,"[10] He was not simply telling the handful of people in attendance to physically follow Him wherever He was going that day. He was instructing all of us who look to Him as the director of our lives to faithfully follow the example He set, the lessons He taught, and the commands He gave. When I attempt to live my life in the attitude and example of Christ, I am living *in His name*. When I appeal to the Father in the name of Jesus, I am asking God to do no more and no less than the very things He has promised to do, under the conditions He has promised to do them. I am placing *myself*, not God, under the obligation and compulsion of Jesus' name.

To find God's "blessing ground," we must live in accordance with what God blesses. In other words, we need to move our lives under the umbrella of His blessing. God doesn't bless sin. God doesn't bless evil. God doesn't bless hate. God doesn't bless pride. God does bless the meek—those who serve others. God does bless those who are hungry and thirsty for His presence. God does bless those who recognize their need for Him in their lives.[11] God's blessing ground is not a hidden or secret place. It requires no passport, just the map of His holy Word. God *wants* us to live blessed lives, so He has given us a road map to follow. Of course, it is of no blessed value sitting on the shelf. Only when we open, read, study, learn, meditate on, and strive to *follow* the guide God has so graciously provided for us can we expect to find—and recognize—God's blessing in our lives.

RECEIVING BLESSING: AWE AND WONDER
There is, of course, one more step in being blessed—*receiving* the blessing. Though it seems an obvious act, it isn't always easy. Children with disabilities can be incredible blessings—but receiving them as such is a difficult step. The loss of a job can be an incredible blessing—but receiving it as such can be frightening. Even illness can sometimes be a blessing—but receiving it as such can seem plain foolish or masochistic! The truth is, we define blessing in temporary and, most often, physical terms: wealth, health, comfort, prestige, power. But God's greatest blessings are rarely defined that way. God wants to give us better things—things that transform our lives into objects of eternal, heavenly beauty and lasting significance.

More than two thousand years ago, God told a young virgin teenager that He was going to turn her life upside down. Though she was engaged to be married to a local carpenter, God was going to make her pregnant before the wedding! How would we expect her to receive this news? She would be an outcast, her wedding plans would be significantly altered (no doubt that new wedding gown wasn't going to fit much longer), and who was going to believe that the father of her baby was the Holy Spirit? But wait; let's look down the road a bit. What lay ahead in her future? This same baby who had completely dashed all the plans she and her boyfriend had made would grow up to be ridiculed, rejected, falsely accused, tortured, and publicly executed in one of the most inhumane deaths ever devised by man. Now which one of us would quickly jump up to claim *that* blessing?

Yet look at Mary's reply to the angel Gabriel when he brought her this "good news": "I am the Lord's servant. May everything you have said about me come true."[12] What looked like tragic circumstances were in fact the incredible implementation of God's plan of salvation.

To receive God's unexpected blessings, we must be *available* for Him to bless—living in His blessing ground, looking for, and forward to, His presence and power in our midst. Then we must be ready and willing to receive what He is holding out to us—whether or not we understand it, whether or not it feels good, even whether or not it makes sense at the moment. This requires complete trust and faith that if it's from God, it is therefore good, and if it's good, God will fulfill His promises and purposes through and in it. It sometimes means giving up every one of our own plans and hanging on for dear life. But in the end, we will join Mary's celebration song:

> *Oh, how my soul praises the Lord.*
> *How my spirit rejoices in God my Savior!*
> *For he took notice of his lowly servant girl,*
> *and from now on all generations will call me blessed.*
> *For the Mighty One is holy,*
> *and he has done great things for me.*[13]

TRANSFORMATION

The ultimate and greatest result of God's blessing is transformation. It's not merely alteration but a *character conversion* in us, a metamorphosis from one state to another—from despair to hope, fear to joy, weakness to strength. Not a changing of who we are, but a transformation into who we were created to be. Not a loss of identity, but a newfound strength and power within our identity. God wants to take us beyond our heavy, burdensome, merely physical existence to the fuller, powerfully delicate, and profoundly significant spiritual core of who God planned us to be.

Transformation is like what happens to water when heat and tea leaves are added. If the water is removed from the heat too soon or the leaves are not left in long enough, the result is a weak, barely drink- able solution. We may add sugar and cream to disguise its flavor and distract our taste buds, but they only cover up the weak, bitter taste. This substance cannot satisfy our desire for the rich, full beverage we were craving. But if the water is allowed to come to a boil and the leaves are left in long enough, the water is changed into something rich, soothing, and warming. The water has been transformed! The water still has its same elemental identity—it is still made up of two molecules hydrogen, one oxygen—but it is no longer just water, and it isn't just water with leaves in it. It has *become* tea. It has become what it was intended to be when it was poured into the pot. The leaves and the heat are the blessings that God adds to the water of our lives. They are the elements that bring about the transformation God wants to work in us. They are the path and reward of God's *better* plan for us!

USEFUL VESSELS: BEING BLESSED TRANSFORMS THE PURPOSE OF YOUR LIFE

God uses His blessings to transform us from mere inhabitants of this planet to stewards of history. The history of the universe has its beginning and eventual ending in God's plan, and all time is marching forward to the fulfillment of that history. It began with Him, and it will end with Him. He has given us the privilege to participate in the amazing unfolding and narration of "His story" during our lifetimes. Our roles are largely cast by how much we desire to be used by and be useful for the Author.

Shakespeare wrote, "All the world's a stage, and all the men and women merely players."[14] But far from being merely a playwright for the amusement of the ages, God is the sculptor of destiny and providence. He is the designer of lives and a potter of people. He forms each one of us into His unique patterns and creates every individual life for His specific purpose. Each of us is a precious and fragile vessel, created by the loving and attentive touch of the Creator Himself. The prophet Isaiah wrote, "LORD, you are our Father. We are the clay, and you are the potter. We all are formed by your hand."[15] And when He breathes His breath of life into us, when we take that first gulp of earthly air, He gives us the gift of choice. We can choose to remain His vessels and accomplish the purpose for which we were created, or we can choose to go our own path—to attempt to achieve with our own power a place of significance in this life.

The more we live the kind of lives God blesses, the more open we are to receiving God's blessings, and the more our lives are transformed into something God can use to fulfill His purposes. My time on earth is no longer simply a series of events that fill the gap from birth to death. It is transformed into an effective and important role in the fulfillment of God's universal and eternal plan.

LIKENESS OF CHRIST: BEING BLESSED TRANSFORMS YOU

God's blessings do not just affect the circumstances of my life; they also work together with the Holy Spirit to transform the essence of who I am. Scripture tells us that the primary work of the Spirit in us is to glorify Christ by transforming us into His image. God chose each one of us to become like His Son; being a Christian means becoming a new person. A new life has begun for us, a life in which the Spirit of God Himself renews our thoughts and attitudes.[16] "Where the Spirit of the Lord is, there is freedom. And we, who with unveiled faces all reflect the Lord's glory, are being transformed into his likeness with ever-increasing glory, which comes from the Lord, who is the Spirit." [17]

God transforms us by changing the way we think. As we connect with God through prayer and Scripture, we gain the ability to know what God wants us to do and to understand how good and pleasing and perfect His plan is for our lives.[18] Our perspectives, priorities, and preferences are transformed from earthly viewpoints to divine perception. Through His Spirit in us, we can actually develop Christlike attitudes and wisdom[19]—the pure, peace-seeking, gentle, willing, and meek wisdom of Jesus—lived in an attitude of mercy and goodness and sincerity.[20] We *become* (not merely behave like) men and women of peace, joy, and gratitude; we *become* (not simply act) compassionate, merciful, and loving. We *become* the people we were created to be.

God's blessings are His daily reminders that He is with us; they are His affirmations that we are on the right track, that we are walking the path He has set for us. God's blessings are also the method of holy transformation. They mold our lives into beautiful, effective vessels for the Creator, carrying history to its glorious finale. Living God's *better* plan means living in constant expectancy of His blessing. Each moment is pregnant with potential grace, the promise of wonder, and ceaseless joy! God has planned a life of blessing and fulfillment for each one of us, but we must allow ourselves to be available for that plan and be willing to be transformed by it.

> "For I know the plans I have for you," says the LORD.
> "They are plans for good and not for disaster, to give
> you a future and a hope. In those days when you pray, I
> will listen. If you look for me wholeheartedly, you will
> find me. I will be found by you," says the LORD.[21]

QUESTIONS

Honestly consider your definition of being blessed. Evaluate your definition in light of what you know about God's purposes, plans, and ways.

Keeping a daily journal or a list of the blessings we see each day helps us to become more aware of God's handiwork in our lives. Consider keeping your own "Blessings Journal" for a month. Note how your awareness of God's working in your life grows as you begin to look for, expect, and recognize evidence of His presence each day.

God has given us His Word as a guidebook for living a blessed life. Are you living on (or in close proximity to) God's "blessing grounds"? Are you readily available and willing for God's blessings? Prayerfully consider what steps you may need to take to come more into alignment with the type of life God blesses.

7

Dedicate Everything to Christ

WALKING THE PATH

Whatever you do, whether in word or deed, do it all in the name of the Lord
Jesus, giving thanks to God the Father through him.
COLOSSIANS 3:17 (NIV)

GIVING IT YOUR ALL

Greg and I both enjoy coming from large families. Greg is the third of
five kids and I am the fourth of five, so aiming for five children had
always been our dream. In the spring of 1981, we decided we were
ready for another child. We went back to FCVN. After the fall of
Vietnam, the agency had changed its name to *Friends of Children of Various
Nations* and was working primarily with Korean agencies. They
told us about a little boy named Han, who had a skin disorder called
ichthyosis. We were given pictures and told to consult with doctors
about his condition before deciding. Of course, as soon as we saw his
darling little face, we knew instantly what our answer would be. But
we obediently sought out two dermatologists for their advice and
opinions. Ichthyosis is a rare genetic disorder of the skin, causing
moderate to severe scaling. There is no cure, and daily treatment is
necessary. The scales can result in serious lesions, infections, and

scarring. After looking at his pictures, the doctors agreed that Han's whole body was affected, and the prognosis was that as he got older (and I'm not joking here) the scaling would "get better, get worse, or stay the same." We called the agency and started the paperwork to get Han home. We named him Nicholas Han.

Nick and Nori were only three months apart in age, and they bonded quickly—even inventing their own language that they would interpret for the benefit of others. When Jesus said, "Blessed are the peacemakers, for they shall be called the sons of God,"[1] He must have had Nick in mind. From the day of his arrival, Nick made it his goal to promote peace in our home—even if it meant taking the blame for things he didn't do.

Quite unexpectedly, less than a year after Nick arrived, I saw a picture of a little boy in a monthly adoption newsletter we subscribed to. The caption explained that he was in Korea and needed a permanent home. I couldn't explain it, but the moment I saw his picture, I felt that I was looking at one of my own children. It turns out I was! The little boy, Jae, had significant physical anomalies, so I took the picture to our friends at FCVN and had them inquire about him. We were sent X-rays, and because of the severity of his problems, we were encouraged to take his records to Children's Hospital in Denver for consultation. They diagnosed him with arthrogryposis, a rare joint/muscle syndrome. His toes, feet, knees, fingers, hands, elbows, and shoulder joints were all either malformed or missing entirely. We were told that he probably would never walk (we'd heard that before), that he probably would not be able to feed himself or write, and that his potential would be pretty limited (we'd heard that too). The doctor couldn't imagine why anybody would voluntarily take on such a problem, but we knew that this child wasn't a problem; he was God's special gift and most assuredly a Henk.

Three months later, Christopher Jae arrived home. We had been told that he was three years old, and we knew that he was significantly physically challenged, so we weren't sure what to expect when we picked him up at the airport. As we had done before, we greeted his arrival with friends and family in attendance at the Denver airport. We weren't sure if he'd be able to walk the long concourse—and we were right. He couldn't walk it—he *ran* it! It was all we could do to keep up with him. Apparently no one had ever told him that he shouldn't be able to use his legs!

We lived in a tri-level house at the time, and when we got home, it was clear that this little boy had never gone up or down stairs on his own before. The four other kids ran upstairs, excited to show their new brother his bed and toys, and Chris laboriously struggled up the first few steps. Although we knew that eventually he would have to conquer this mountain, he didn't need to do it on his first night home, so Greg scooped Chris up in his arms and carried him to the top of the staircase. Chris wiggled out of Greg's grip and rattled off a line in Korean that we were sure we *didn't* want translated. Then Chris scooted down the entire staircase on his belly and started with step one all over again! By the end of the night, he had conquered every staircase in the house. It was a preview of the very determined personality we had just added to our clan.

We had our five kids! Michelle was six, Josh was five, and Nick, Nori, and Chris were all three years old. Over time, Chris exceeded all expectations. Ever resourceful and determined, he created ways to feed himself, dress himself, write, draw, and eventually even drive!

All five of our children had continuing surgeries until their teens, sometimes augmented by physical, occupational, or speech therapy. Yet strangely, our family felt pretty normal—at least to us! The kids played soccer and took piano lessons, ballet lessons, ice skating lessons, *drum* lessons (what were we thinking?)—all the normal things. We saw more doctors and had more specialists than the average family, and we definitely drew stares when we went out, but that was just part of who we were.

A year later FCVN called us again. There was a thirteen-year-old girl in a Korean orphanage in urgent need of a home. She was growing too old to stay in the orphanage, and the agency was hoping to find a family for her as quickly as possible. Of course we couldn't say no. So, shortly before her fourteenth birthday, our last child, Suzanne, joined the Henk family. In many ways she was the one we were the least prepared to parent. Traveling halfway around the world to a country she'd never been to that speaks a language she didn't know, to join a family she'd never met must surely have been one of the most frightening things imaginable. Then to suddenly be thrust into the role of the *oldest* of six children added yet additional pressure and dismay. Unfortunately, Suzanne was the only one in the scenario who had no say in the matter. Although we had been led to believe that she had chosen us as much as we had chosen her to be a part of our family, she in fact was never really given much of a choice. The decision to be uprooted from the only life she had ever known, be transported to Denver, and placed in our home and family was one made for her, not by her.

We also did not realize how different the needs of a teenager *coming into* a family were from the needs of a teenager *growing up* in the family. Her teenage years were understandably complicated, yet she grew into a beautiful and accomplished young woman. An honor student, she learned quickly and took pride in her accomplishments. She excelled in everything she put her mind to and developed into a competent and self-confident adult. In all, Suzanne really only lived with us for little more than four years, from fourteen to eighteen, when she left for college, but that was enough to weave her into the Henk family tapestry!

If adopting a teenager showed us that we weren't prepared for adolescent parenting, having five children reach their hormonal heights at the same time confirmed it. Shortly after Suzanne went off to college, and in the midst of Joshua's turmoil, Greg's job moved to California. It was a trying move for everyone, but most of all for the boys. Both Michelle and Nori excelled in school, so they were able to channel their emotional transitions into scholastic achievement. Nick had hated school since preschool, and I realize now that he probably should have been homeschooled. The social and academic pressures were always difficult for him; he was a boy who loved being home and everything that home entailed. He was always my best helper and companion. The combination of moving to a new school and the pressures at home that were building around Josh and his problems conspired against Nick. His one outlet was soccer. As a fearless competitor on the field, it was playing soccer that kept him in school year after year (and summer school after summer school).

Chris struggled with a school system that was both unsympathetic and unbending when it came to meeting his physical challenges. Our school district in Denver had been incredibly responsive to the physical, intellectual, and social needs of its students. All our children had benefited from special resources programs, but now we found ourselves in a district that not only withheld mandated resources but also penalized students with special needs. We found out months later that Chris's sixth-grade teacher made him sit outside of the classroom because he physically couldn't keep up with the other kids. Chris has only one hand and is missing the muscles, tendons, and joints in his arms. Amazingly, he *did* figure out a way to write, but it took him much longer than others to complete written exams. This frustrated his teacher, and instead of offering him the option of oral exams (as was mandated on his special resource contract), she simply sat him outside and ordered him to work on his own.

This was not the first, nor would it be the last, challenge in Chris's life, but he handled it in his God-given nature—head on! It was months before we realized what was happening since Chris was determined to manage on his own. When we did find out, Greg and I were furious and wanted him immediately transferred to another class, but Chris objected. He told us that God put him in that classroom to teach the teacher about kids with disabilities. How could he change classes before she learned that everyone deserves a chance? He felt that he had an obligation to the *next* kid with disabilities she would teach. Of course, we intervened (with the principal and our lawyer) to make sure that Chris would no longer be subjected to such demoralizing treatment, but he did finish the year victoriously!

Being the "handicapped kid" in school is never easy. Often on the fringe, rarely in the mainstream; popular on campus, but rarely invited to parties; known by many, companion to few—it's a tough road even under the best circumstances. But Chris taught our whole family that the way we face our experiences can have a lasting impact not only on our lives, but on others as well, if we choose to dedicate these experiences to God's purposes. When we determine to "do it all in the name of the Lord Jesus,"[2] we realize that today's challenges are tomorrow's victories and we can give thanks to God in the midst of what we are facing. Today Chris lives independently in his own apartment and works for a Mercedes dealership. And even though he has a driver's license (another obstacle that doctors thought he would never overcome), the boy we were told would probably never walk not only walks miles each day by choice but also skis and plays soccer! He continues to inspire those around him with his tenacious and creative resourcefulness, and he sees the challenges in his life as possibilities, not obstacles.

Ecclesiastes 3:1 says that "there is a time for everything, and a season for every activity under heaven."[3] As surely as day follows night and summer follows spring, the days turn into weeks, and months turn into years. Time passes, children grow, crises resolve, lessons are learned. Over the years our family has discovered that God *does* have a unique plan for each one of our lives. His plans put us on pathways that are far better, yet often harder, than anything we would ever plan for ourselves. But we must walk that path if we are going to claim its blessings! All our kids are on their own path now, finding God's dream for their lives.

After college, Suzanne pursued a prestigious career in computer systems analysis for engineering firms, and she has an avid love for anything outdoors—biking, skiing, hiking. We were delighted when Suzanne married Andy, a wonderful, kind hydrogeologist who shares her love for nature and travel. When the kids were young, many of our family vacations were camping trips. Greg taught all the kids how to pitch a tent, hike safely, and fish, as well as some basic rock climbing skills; and of course all our kids learned to ski while we lived in Denver.

Michelle became a beautiful, sensitive, gifted elementary school teacher. When she met and eventually married Teddy, we knew that God had brought this wonderful young man into our family. Michelle, our first child, was also the first to bless us with a grandchild. Savannah was born the day after Christmas—what a gift! Being a grandparent is teaching me yet another aspect of God's love. Christ called our heavenly Father *Abba*,[4] meaning "Papa," an endearing title. The first time I laid eyes on our precious little granddaughter, my heart was filled with a new kind of love—an utterly accepting love, one that wholly delights in this precious little child. With the perspective that comes from having raised a family already, I find that being a grandparent is for me a more relaxed, patient love. I have come to believe that the spirit of *Abba* is a lot like that of a grandparent.

Josh and Meghan are following their path at Daybreak in Canada. Answering our prayers better than we could have hoped, Meghan's family has become one of our greatest blessings. Josh worked with her mother before he ever knew Meghan, so when they became engaged, his mother-in-law called to tell me that not only were they thrilled that Josh was joining their family but that *she* had loved Josh before Meghan did! How blessed to know that my son is still surrounded by loving family, even so far away from our home.

Nick never did warm up to the concept of school, but with God's help, he did graduate. At nineteen he began his career in construction, where he truly found his niche. Working in inspecting and material testing, Nick, still the peacemaker, often works as a mediator between the contractor and the project owner. The job also gives him the opportunity to travel around the country working on different projects. While he was in Arkansas, he met Polly, a gifted artist, and settled down to raise a family. Nick and Polly have given us our first precious grandson, Gabriel. We have discovered that God's dream for our lives just continues to grow and get better. Each new chapter, each new addition, each new generation offers its own challenges, blessings, and opportunities to discover a deeper understanding of how good and wonderful and loving our Abba is.

Our daughter Nori has blossomed into a remarkable young woman. Her early difficulties made her a tenacious goal setter and gave her a thirst for growth, knowledge, and accomplishment. It is amazing to think back to when she first arrived in our family and how God poured His life-changing power and love into her little body. Nori grew in joy, love, grace, and courage, and although—or perhaps because—she faced numerous surgeries and struggled with residual pain from her damaged joints, she developed a heart for the struggles of others. At the end of her first mission trip to Mexico at age thirteen, she committed her life to bringing the message of Christ's love to others. She told us later that on the last night of the trip, when the speaker asked who might be considering dedicating their lives to missions, she thought, *Who would choose such a difficult calling?* only to find herself one of the people to stand up. She said there was no doubt that the power of the Holy Spirit had brought her to her feet. Nori has continued to follow her calling of bringing the heart of Christ to the disenfranchised of this world. She is currently working on her PhD in sociology, having already earned a master's degree in theology.

One night years ago, we watched a television documentary about genetic engineering. After it was over I asked Nori, who was thirteen at the time, how she felt about the subject. What if science could have made it possible for her to have been born without her birth defects? She looked at me and said, "You don't understand. These things have shaped me to be who I am and who I am meant to be."

When Nori was young, I used to scoop her up in my arms and ask, "Why do I love you so much?" She would answer, "Because I'm the best little thing that ever happened to you!" What joy is found in God's blessings! The psalmist exclaimed, "You crown the year with a bountiful harvest; even the hard pathways overflow with abundance."[5] The pathway to blessing isn't promised to be an easy road, just the best road. God has crowned our lives with amazing bounty, and the harder the pathway, the more abundant His blessing.

When we believe that God is good and that His agenda is better than ours—when we determine to face the realities of our lives, change our perspectives, and endeavor to see things from God's point of view—our journeys through this life become paths of blessing. God's dream for all of us is to walk those paths in such a way that the people around us will also see how good He is!

DEDICATING EVERYTHING TO CHRIST

The Bible verse I have clung to all these years, Luke 1:45, says, "Blessed is she who has believed." The blessing always begins with believing, but the blessing multiplies when we dedicate our lives to Christ for His glory, His use, and His purposes. It was God who brought each child into our home. It was He who planned their lives and gave Greg and me the privilege of having our lives intertwined with theirs. It was He who provided for our every need, who showed us how to continue through the dark times and how to celebrate in the good times. The greatest blessing of all was not having our troubles and tribulations removed or solved for us but having the Lord of the universe walk through them with us. Immanuel—*God with us!* God has promised us:

Do not be afraid, for I have ransomed you. I have called you by name; you are mine. When you go through deep

waters, I will be with you. When you go through rivers
of difficulty, you will not drown. When you walk
through the fire of oppression, you will not be burned
up; the flames will not consume you. For I am the LORD,
your God, the Holy One of Israel, your Savior.[6]

God asks us to honor Him on our journeys so that the world
around us will see His love and come to know His goodness as well.
We honor God by dedicating our lives to Christ, Immanuel.[7] And we
dedicate our lives to Christ by giving Him the two things He desires
most: our love and our service.

LOVE COMPLETELY

The love we give to and receive from God weaves our lives into a
beautiful cycle of faith. The more we love God, the more we will
depend on Him and trust Him to use our lives for His plan and purposes. As we experience the complete sufficiency and abundance of
His love, we will love Him even more. Jesus told us,

> The most important commandment is this: "Listen,
> O Israel! The LORD our God is the one and only LORD.
> And you must love the LORD your God with all your
> heart, all your soul, all your mind, and all your strength."[8]

- When we attempt to love God, who is *Love*, with all our
  hearts—to love Him more than anything or anyone else, to
  love Him more than comfort or possession or pleasure—then
  our hearts will begin to accept the love that God is pouring
  into us. We will begin to experience the freedom to love others
  without fear of rejection.
- When we attempt to love God, who is *Truth*, with all our minds
  and understanding—to accept His Word as the one and only
  standard of absolute truth, to respect His wisdom more than

our opinions—then our minds will begin to grasp the
significance of God's perfect plan for us. We will begin to
experience freedom from the fear of being misunderstood by
others.

- When we attempt to love God, who is *Life*, with all our souls,
attitudes, emotions, and motives—to submit our will to His
will—then we will begin to grow in spiritual maturity. The
Holy Spirit will produce in us the quality of character that
transforms God's love into fruitful priorities and perspectives,
and we will begin to experience freedom from the fear of being
judged by others.

- When we attempt to love God, who is the *Sustainer of Life*, with
all our strength, with every decision we make, with every
action we take and each word we speak, then we will become
strengthened by the outpouring of His endlessly abundant provision and providence. We will be able to openly give and
receive encouragement, care, and love from others, free from
the fear of becoming diminished, drained, or dominated.

When we willingly determine to love God as much as we possibly
can, the love that is given and received back begins to overcome the
fears and shadows in our lives. We will realize that:

> God is love, and all who live in love live in God, and
> God lives in them. And as we live in God, our love grows
> more perfect. . . . Such love has no fear, because perfect
> love expels all fear.[9]

We receive God's love through loving Him. The more we are filled
with His love, the more we are freed to love others. Free to give without expecting in return because God will give us all we need. Free to
serve without fear of rejection because God will never reject us. Free to

risk relationship and vulnerability without fear of being misunderstood because God knows and cares about our deepest thoughts and feelings.

SERVE UNPRETENTIOUSLY

Jesus said, "I am giving you a new commandment: Love each other. Just as I have loved you, you should love each other. Your love for one another will prove to the world that you are my disciples."[10]

At the end of His earthly life, Jesus met with His disciples to celebrate the Passover.

> He got up from the table, took off his robe, wrapped a towel around his waist, and poured water into a basin. Then he began to wash the disciples' feet, drying them with the towel he had around him. . . . After washing their feet, he put on his robe again and sat down and asked, "Do you understand what I was doing? You call me 'Teacher' and 'Lord,' and you are right, because that's what I am. And since I, your Lord and Teacher, have washed your feet, you ought to wash each other's feet. I have given you an example to follow. Do as I have done to you. I tell you the truth, slaves are not greater than their master. Nor is the messenger more important than the one who sends the message. Now that you know these things, God will bless you for doing them."[11]

Jesus told us that the path of blessing is to serve others from a position of brokenness—from our knees, as servants. We do it not for glory or praise, not for power or prestige, not for profit or gain. Instead, we serve because we have been served by God's plans for our good and by His faithfulness to complete those plans. God has put us on a path that He has promised to travel with us. A path where He provides for every need and hardship we may encounter. It is a path that leads to a greater plan than our own agendas, a path of greater purpose than our own desires, and a path that will yield greater significance than we can imagine. When we realize that our lives are tied to *that* path and that it is for God's greatest glory that we are on that road, then we are free to claim the path for ourselves. It is a path of blessing unequaled by any reward the world can give us. It is a path of servanthood: a life of loving and serving God by loving and serving others.

The path of servanthood is the intentional practice of putting others' needs above our own because we have confidence that our Father is taking care of us. It means reaching out and giving to others because we realize that our precious Lord gave everything for us. We are blessed by letting go of our own worries because we believe in God's promise that He will not forget us or forget to provide for us. Jesus told His followers:

> That is why I tell you not to worry about everyday life—
> whether you have enough food to eat or enough clothes
> to wear. For life is more than food, and your body more
> than clothing. Look at the ravens. They don't plant or
> harvest or store food in barns, for God feeds them. And
> you are far more valuable to him than any birds! Can all
> your worries add a single moment to your life? And if
> worry can't accomplish a little thing like that, what's the
> use of worrying over bigger things? Look at the lilies and
> how they grow. They don't work or make their clothing,
> yet Solomon in all his glory was not dressed as beauti-
> fully as they are. And if God cares so wonderfully for
> flowers that are here today and thrown into the fire
> tomorrow, he will certainly care for you. Why do you
> have so little faith? And don't be concerned about what
> to eat and what to drink. Don't worry about such things.
> These things dominate the thoughts of unbelievers all

over the world, but your Father already knows your
needs. Seek the Kingdom of God above all else, and he
will give you everything you need. So don't be afraid, little flock. For it gives your Father great happiness to give
you the Kingdom. Sell your possessions and give to
those in need. This will store up treasure for you in
heaven! And the purses of heaven never get old or
develop holes. Your treasure will be safe; no thief can
steal it and no moth can destroy it. Wherever your treasure is, there the desires of your heart will also be."[12]

Because we can have confidence in God's constant and sufficient
provision for our lives, we are free to care about others, about their
needs, and about what we can do to provide for them. The Bible tells us
that true faith expresses itself in love[13] and that the kind of religion God
wants from us is to care for the weak and hungry, the needy and those
in trouble, the unloved, the hurting, the poor, and the oppressed.[14] God
told Isaiah that the kind of fasting (religious discipline and practice) He
wants from us is to:

Free those who are wrongly imprisoned; lighten the burden of those who work for you. Let the oppressed go
free, and remove the chains that bind people. Share your
food with the hungry, and give shelter to the homeless.
Give clothes to those who need them, and do not hide
from relatives who need your help.[15]

Jesus told us that when we feed the hungry, clothe the homeless,
visit the lonely, and care about those who are imprisoned, it is the
same to God as if we were feeding, clothing, and caring for Jesus
Himself![16] And in return, God has told us that when we care about the
weak and helpless, when we reach out and help those who are in trouble, He will bless us and make our lives a blessing to others.

Your light will shine out from the darkness, and the
darkness around you will be as bright as noon. The LORD
will guide you continually, giving you water when you
are dry and restoring your strength. You will be like a
well-watered garden, like an ever-flowing spring.[17]

The path of blessing is not an easy path; it is not a comfortable
path; it is not a particularly prestigious or pretty path. But it is a *better*
path, a *blessed* path, and a *beautiful* path—it's the path traveled with the
Lord God Himself. It is a path of sorrows, walked with the Man of
Sorrows;[18] it is a path of brokenness, shared with the broken Bread of
Life;[19] it is a path of victory and triumph, celebrated with the trium-
phant King Himself![20]

SANCTIFICATION

The moment we recognize Jesus Christ as Lord of our lives and accept
His sacrifice as the only provision for our eternal salvation, we are
completely reconciled with God, restored to the relationship with
Him that we were created to enjoy, and welcomed into His Kingdom
with joy and celebration. As our renewed relationship with the Creator of the universe develops, our lives are increasingly blessed and
we are increasingly set apart for God's use. We grow in our service to
and love for God, and our priorities and perspectives are gradually
transformed by the work of His Spirit in us. We find ourselves becoming more vital, more fully alive and purposeful, and we begin to
realize the urgency of using our lives for God's purposes. We become
sanctified—set apart for God's use and God's blessing. We are God's
ambassadors to the world, and the attitudes, perspective, and priorities of Christ become progressively more evident in our lives. We
exhibit the attitudes of gratitude and joy, the perspective of the
sacred Kingdom of God, and the priority of glorifying Christ in all
things.

GRATITUDE AND JOY

It is impossible to separate gratitude and joy. A thankful heart is a joyful heart, and a heart filled with joy produces gratitude. Joy is different from happiness. Happiness is a temporary condition, brought on and diminished by circumstances and events. For example, chocolate makes me happy, but the absence of chocolate takes away my happiness. Fitting into my new jeans makes me happy; busting the seams of my favorite jeans takes away my happiness. But joy is a condition of the heart. It is an "attitude of gratitude"—an awareness of God's presence among us; a recognition of God's amazing and totally undeserved love for us; and an excited, childlike anticipation of what wonder-filled thing He is going to do next. Joy is also a choice, and we can choose to develop a willingness of heart that empowers joyfulness in our lives.

The key to joy is praise and thanksgiving. Thankful praise is a powerful secret weapon in our spiritual armory. When we praise God with thankfulness—no matter what is happening in our lives, no matter how we are feeling, and no matter how things appear to us—it actually effects change! *We* change—our attitudes, our outlooks, our motivations, and our perceptions. But this is no mere trick to make us feel better; it is not some psychological strategy or maneuver to be taken lightly. Praising God in all circumstances is a command. It is a demonstration of our faith that God is sovereign over all things, including every circumstance, condition, and event of our lives. The Bible tells us that we are to "always [give] thanks to God the Father for everything, in the name of our Lord Jesus Christ."[21] It doesn't say to give thanks if we feel like it or when we are happy; it says to *always* give thanks to God for *everything*.

The truth is that gratitude changes circumstances. The sorrowful arrival of a child with disabilities can be transformed into the celebration of an incredible blessing. The downward spiral of depression and despair can be turned around to a path of healing and strength. The

self-destructive path of sin and rebellion can become the very preparation for a life of service and blessing. I know these examples firsthand! They are not theory; they are fact—proven in my own life.

But practically speaking, how do we do this? How do we thank
God when, frankly, we are angry with Him? How do we praise God
when we feel nothing but despair? How is it possible to glorify God
when we are in a state of brokenness? The Bible says to "fix your
thoughts on what is true, and honorable, and right, and pure, and
lovely, and admirable. Think about things that are excellent and worthy of praise."[22]

We have personal responsibility in our circumstances. We have
the obligation to take ownership of our condition and to choose,
regardless of how we feel, to obey the directive of thankfulness. God
does not ask us to *feel* thankful, simply to give Him thanks and praise.
God does not reject pitiful beginnings. He delights when we even
begin to attempt to obey Him![23] Even if all we can thank Him for is
that He created gravity so we are not floating out in space, it's a start.

Why does God want us to thank Him? I believe that one reason is
because through our praising and thanking Him, God gets our attention. And once He's gotten our attention He can begin to show us
that we're not alone. He wants to whisper His name into our hearts, to
remind us that He is *Immanuel*—God with us! When we begin to realize that we are not alone, that the Almighty God is with us and for us,
we begin to rely on His assurance and comfort. We experience peace
of mind and heart, which the Bible calls "the peace that transcends all
understanding"—the peace that becomes the foundation of our joy!
No matter what we are going through, when we offer our circumstances to God for His use and when we dedicate the process and the
outcome to the name and glory of Christ, giving thanks to God for
His part, we find ourselves marked by a spirit of joy and an attitude of
thankfulness.

Rejoice in the Lord always. I will say it again: Rejoice!
Let your gentleness be evident to all. The Lord is near.
Do not be anxious about anything, but in everything, by
prayer and petition, with thanksgiving, present your
requests to God. And the peace of God, which transcends all understanding, will guard your hearts and
your minds in Christ Jesus.[24]

SACRED AND HOLY

"You must be holy in everything you do, just as God who chose you is
holy. For the Scriptures say, 'You must be holy because I am holy.'"[25]

The apostle Paul prayed, "May the Lord make your love for one
another and for all people grow and overflow, just as our love for you
overflows. May he, as a result, make your hearts strong, blameless, and
holy as you stand before God our Father when our Lord Jesus comes
again with all his holy people."[26] The concept of holiness conjures up a
variety of visions for us: the sanctimonious, holier-than-thou church
lady who is always looking down her nose at us, judging and criticizing
our every effort, catching and condemning every error; or perhaps the
saints whose life callings seem far superior in self-sacrifice or religious
dedication than we could ever aspire to. We think of the early church
fathers and mothers, the martyrs of our faith, Mother Teresa, the Pope.
But us? We're just regular people! How can God ask us to live holy
lives? That's a pretty daunting order! But in fact, holiness is just the process of regular people living for the purposes of God's Kingdom and
being transformed to reflect God's character as demonstrated by
Christ. Every life on this planet is sacred because it is created by God
for His purpose, it belongs to God by His creation, and it is loved by
God by design. The very first pages of the Bible tell us that human
beings are created in God's own image. That is sacred! When sacred
lives are dedicated back to God, they become holy.

When we acknowledge that we and people around us—every one

of them, whether nice, funny, rich, beautiful, broken, scared, poor, hungry, imprisoned, dying, lost, or lonely—are sacred creations of God, then we begin to grasp the importance of dedicating every minute of our lives, every experience of our existence, and every encounter with another person to God. Each life that God has created has within it the promise of holiness.

> You . . . have been called by God to be his own holy people. He made you holy by means of Christ Jesus, just as he did for all people everywhere who call on the name of our Lord Jesus Christ, their Lord and ours.[27]

GLORIFY CHRIST

> Let the message about Christ, in all its richness, fill your lives. Teach and counsel each other with all the wisdom he gives. Sing psalms and hymns and spiritual songs to God with thankful hearts. And whatever you do or say, do it as a representative of the Lord Jesus, giving thanks through him to God the Father.[28]

The ultimate step in finding, accepting, and living God's *better* plan for your life is dedicating everything to the purpose of glorifying Christ. There is no higher calling; there is no greater achievement; there is no more significant accomplishment, than bringing tribute and honor to the One who has redeemed us. By His shed blood and sacrificed life, He has made it possible for us to have two lives: eternal life in the heavenly Kingdom of God and an earthly life lived for the purposes and fulfillment of that Kingdom.

The psalmist tells us that by its very nature, all of God's creation declares His glory.[29] The book of Revelation affirms that at the end of history, every creature in heaven and on earth will declare and sing the glory of Christ.[30] We have the opportunity not only to live a blessed life—designed, purposed, and empowered by a loving and attentive heavenly Father—but to honor Him in the process of living out that plan. We glorify God through Christ by dedicating all our assets, capabilities, plans, talents, and dreams to His use. We allow Him to use them as He designs, how He determines, and for His own good purposes. In that way, the process as well as the outcome of our lives will inspire others to look to God and find His better plan for their lives as well.

> God has given each of you a gift from his great variety of
> spiritual gifts. Use them well to serve one another. Do
> you have the gift of speaking? Then speak as though
> God himself were speaking through you. Do you have
> the gift of helping others? Do it with all the strength and
> energy that God supplies. Then everything you do will
> bring glory to God through Jesus Christ. All glory and
> power to him forever and ever! Amen.[31]

GREAT COMMISSION

God has chosen to use people as His method of spreading His plan through the ages and throughout the world.[32] It is therefore our honor and responsibility to tell others by our actions, our example, and our words the Good News of God's *best* plan for our lives—the plan of redemption through Christ. Jesus' last instruction to His disciples was to wait for the Holy Spirit (they first received the Holy Spirit on the day of Pentecost; we get it the moment we accept Christ into our lives) and then to spread the gospel message to their homes, neighborhoods, communities, and world. He told His followers that the greatest thing they could do with their lives was to:

> Go and make disciples of all the nations, baptizing them
> in the name of the Father and the Son and the Holy

Spirit. Teach these new disciples to obey all the commands I have given you. And be sure of this: I am with
you always, even to the end of the age.[33]

There is no other name, no other plan in all of creation or throughout all of history by which men and women can once and for all time
enjoy complete communion with God.[34] There are many philosophies
for living productive lives and many theories for living relatively happy
lives. But there is only one plan that has been given to us by the God of
the universe, the Creator of all things, the Alpha and Omega, God
Almighty, Father and Lord of all—and that is the plan of Jesus Christ,
devised from the beginning of creation, executed in AD 30 and available for every man, woman, and child who wants it. The simple truth is
that Christ's death proved to the world that this is the only way to salvation with God. Jesus proved it by His resurrection; He conquered
death. He was publicly executed, buried in a sealed tomb guarded by
Roman soldiers, and yet three days later rose from the dead and
appeared to hundreds of witnesses before returning to heaven![35] This is
not legend; it is truth, attested to by history and martyrdom throughout the ages. The fact that God allowed Jesus to shed His blood and
sacrifice His life is also grim and sobering proof, for if there had been
any other method by which we could be redeemed from sin, then Jesus
would not have died.[36] Only through Christ are we restored to the eternal relationship we were created for; only through Christ are we given
new lives of significance, grace, and blessing.

This means that anyone who belongs to Christ has
become a new person. The old life is gone; a new life has
begun! And all of this is a gift from God, who brought us
back to himself through Christ. And God has given us
this task of reconciling people to him. For God was in
Christ, reconciling the world to himself, no longer

counting people's sins against them. And he gave us this
wonderful message of reconciliation. So we are Christ's
ambassadors; God is making his appeal through us. We
speak for Christ when we plead, "Come back to God!"
For God made Christ, who never sinned, to be the offering for our sin, so that we could be made right with God
through Christ.[37]

The only way your loved ones, your neighbors, and the people you
encounter at the store or on the airplane are going to know about the
wonderful *best plan* of God is if you care enough, if you love God
enough, if you love others enough to tell them! Tell them your story.
Tell them what God can do and has done in your life.

BLESSED IS SHE!

The journey to living God's dream for our lives is the greatest adventure imaginable. Our lives can make an eternal impact when we determine to live for Christ by seeing each event and encounter as
opportunities to love and serve Him. In the end, the blessing God has
given us is nothing less than lives lived in bigger terms, for more meaningful reasons, with greater fulfillment and purpose than we could have
ever planned for ourselves. It is an amazing thing to be part of an eternal plan that is as big as the Kingdom of God itself but also that is God's
dream for each one of us. Dare to walk this path! Trust in God's goodness, accept His agenda, face each day fully seeking His perspective.
Hang on for the blessing, and then give it all back to Christ. Don't
settle for your dreams; God's are eternally better.

QUESTIONS

The greatest commandment tells us to love God with all of our hearts, minds, souls, and strength. Prayerfully spend some time considering the magnitude of this command. How might your present goals or perspectives be altered if you made this command your highest priority?

What area of loving God completely (heart, mind, soul, or strength) is the biggest challenge for you? Why?

Consider what it means to serve God by serving others. Reflect on your willingness to reach out to those in need in your family, your church, your community, or the world.

Ask God to begin to show who He would have you reach out to at this time and how you can demonstrate your love more fully and effectively to those in need.

Prayerfully ask God to help you praise Him, even during the hard and painful things in your life. Ask Him to help you turn your heart and mind fully to His presence and power in those situations.

What impressions do you have regarding the words sacred *and* holy? *As you consider your own life and the lives of those around you, how aware are you of their sacred nature and their potential for holiness? Ask God to help you to respect and honor what is sacred and holy to Him.*

What do you think a life that glorifies Christ would look like? How fully do you think your life glorifies Christ? How important is it to you to glorify Christ in and with your life? Prayerfully ask God to show you ways you can reflect His glory to those around you.

Who in your life needs to hear the Good News of Christ? Begin to pray for God to give you the opportunity to dedicate your life more fully to Him by sharing His Good News with that person.

Conclusion

The Priority of the Plan

God decided in advance to adopt us into his own family by bringing
us to himself through Jesus Christ. This is what he wanted to do,
and it gave him great pleasure.

EPHESIANS 1:5

DOING IT OVER

A few years ago someone asked me a question: If I were given the
chance to go back in time and do it all over again, if God were to grant
my original plans and dreams—to produce babies with no "special
needs," no disabilities, no drug addictions, and to live a quiet, unre-
markable life—would I exchange the life I've lived? At the time, my
answer was, "For me, no. I would *never* give up the blessings God has
given me and the depth of my relationship with Him because of what
I've lived. But if I could have the same kids and take away what *they*
have gone through, if they could be free of 'special needs,' disabilities,
drug addiction, and the pain these things have brought them, I would
change that."

That was then. Today I have a different answer: I would never give
up what God has done in *all* our lives! The dramatic and traumatic
events we've experienced, and the brokenness that came with them,

have been paths of blessing for each one of us. They have shaped us into vessels God has used and blessed for His bigger plan.

I've learned that there is no better place to be than where God has put us. There is no better dream than His for our lives. I can't imagine a more rewarding life than one that expects miracles, that knows from firsthand experience that God is enough.

Paul wrote:

> May you have the power to understand, as all God's people should, how wide, how long, how high, and how deep his love is. May you experience the love of Christ, though it is too great to understand fully. Then you will be made complete with all the fullness of life and power that comes from God.[1]

The kind of understanding that Paul is talking about is *experiential understanding*—the knowledge that comes only from directly observing something. My family has experienced the goodness of God, the power of His love, and the sufficiency of His provision firsthand. I know that God is my comforter because He has comforted me in my despair. I know that God is my refuge and my strength because He has rescued me in my fear and weakness. The Bible tells us that Jesus is called *Immanuel*,[2] which means "God is with us." God is with us in Christ. God sent Jesus to demonstrate the extent of His love for us, and when He returned to the Father, Jesus sent us the Spirit—the breath of God—to live in us and ensure our communion with Him. It is this Spirit at work in us who transforms our broken lives into objects of beauty and worth. And it is this Spirit who guides us to God's dream for our lives!

Michelle and I used to play a little game in which one of us would say, "I love you," and the other would respond, "I love you more." Then the first would reply, "I love you more than the sky." God's abundance is greater than the breadth of the sky and more plentiful than the stars that fill it! In the Old Testament, God assured Abram that even though his wife, Sarai, was barren, he would be a father of nations.

> The LORD took Abram outside and said to him, "Look up into the sky and count the stars if you can. That's how many descendants you will have!"[3]

Then Scripture says that Abram believed the Lord, and the Lord declared him righteous because of his faith.[4] *Blessed are those who believe!*

THE POWER OF GOD'S PLAN

What has been my purpose for writing this book? If I have a "life message," it is to trust in the goodness of God and to have faith in His greater plan for our lives. But what is that greater plan, and how do we know if we're settling for less? I have come to believe that God's "greater plan" goes far beyond our individual lives. It began in eternity and exists in eternity. Long before we were born we were a part of God's plan, and long after we are gone from this earth we will still exist in His plan.

The graciousness—and awe-fullness—of God is that He has allowed us to accept or deny His plan for our lives. To not intentionally accept God's gift of salvation through Christ is to reject it. The tragedy I see among believers is that so many people who have accepted God's eternal plan of salvation miss the significance of beginning their eternal lives *now*. They don't realize the potential of the relationship that the Creator of the universe has provided for them. They miss their pathway of blessing because they are distracted, discouraged, or damaged by the lies of this world.

The world's messages are loud and distracting—they lure us with the promise of pleasure from things, power, or people. But pleasure is fleeting and leaves us unsatisfied. We become discouraged by our constant efforts to attain more: more things, more comfort, more prestige, more success, more influence, more friends. But in the end, the more we have, the more we long for and the more we find ourselves being controlled by our fear of losing the things we have acquired. And so God has provided for us a better message, a better hope, a better plan—a plan that existed before time, a plan to redeem His beloved children from the mess we have made of our lives and of His creation, and a plan that enables us to live better, more meaningful, and more significant lives now!

As the time for Christ to be glorified approached, He went to a private place to prepare for what He was going to face. The Gospel writers give us a glimpse of the most incredible scene that this planet has ever witnessed: the heart of God the Son crying out to the heart of God the Father.

> They went to the olive grove called Gethsemane, and
> Jesus said, "Sit here while I go and pray." He took Peter,
> James, and John with him, and he became deeply
> troubled and distressed. He told them, "My soul is
> crushed with grief to the point of death. Stay here and
> keep watch with me." He went on a little farther and fell
> to the ground. He prayed that, if it were possible, the
> awful hour awaiting him might pass him by. "Abba,
> Father," he cried out, "everything is possible for you.
> Please take this cup of suffering away from me. Yet
> I want your will to be done, not mine."[5]

> One of the twelve disciples . . . arrived with a crowd of
> men armed with swords and clubs. . . . "Put away your
> sword," Jesus told him. "Those who use the sword will die
> by the sword. Don't you realize that I could ask my Father

for thousands of angels to protect us, and he would send
them instantly? But if I did, how would the Scriptures be
fulfilled that describe what must happen now?"[6]

God had the power to rescue Jesus, but the fulfillment of God's plan
was more important. There are so many times in my life when I have
asked God, "Why? I know you have the power to remove this, to cure
this, to make things better. Why don't you use that power for me in my
pain?" Yet the message from this passage is clear: God's plan is the
supreme priority and the greatest good in all circumstances. We can't
always know how our daily lives fit into the grand scheme of God's
amazing grace, but the whole of Scripture clearly reveals one message.
God's love is not arbitrary, God's power is not random, and God's provision is not capricious. His love is supreme, His power absolute, and
His provision totally sufficient. And that is the greater plan! "Thy will
be done" is not a cop-out or a loophole; it is a statement of our submission to the divine good. It's a statement of intent. We determine to
believe that God's eternal goodness reigns, regardless of our feelings or
our temporary perception of the results.

- The plan has existed from eternity past.
  "Even before he made the world, God loved us and chose
  us in Christ to be holy and without fault in his eyes. *God
  decided in advance to adopt us into his own family by bringing us to
  himself through Jesus Christ.* This is what he wanted to do, and
  it gave him great pleasure. . . . God has now revealed to us
  his mysterious plan regarding Christ, a plan to fulfill his
  own good pleasure."[7]

- God's provision and power have ensured the inevitable
  progression of the plan.
  "He makes everything work out according to his plan."[8]

- The presence of God sustains and assures us while we wait for the fulfillment of the plan.
  "All praise to God, the Father of our Lord Jesus Christ, who has *blessed us with every spiritual blessing in the heavenly realms* because we are united with Christ. . . . So we praise God for the glorious grace he has poured out on us who belong to his dear Son. He is so rich in kindness and grace that he purchased our freedom with the blood of his Son and forgave our sins. *He has showered his kindness on us, along with all wisdom and understanding. . . .* And now you Gentiles have also heard the truth, the Good News that God saves you. And when you believed in Christ, he identified you as his own by *giving you the Holy Spirit,* whom he promised long ago. *The Spirit is God's guarantee* that he will give us the inheritance he promised and that he has purchased us to be his own people."[9]

- The plan will advance until its completion and fulfillment.
  "At the right time he will bring everything together under the authority of Christ—everything in heaven and on earth."[10]

If we are intentional about embracing God's better plan for our lives, we can begin to grasp the potential that God has designed for us—right now, today! The potential of living BLESSED.

Believe in God's goodness, regardless of the circumstances of your life.

Let go of your own agenda. Allow God to plan a better life for you.

Embrace reality. Accept the truth of your life, and let God use it for His purposes.

See with God's heart. Train yourself to look at life through God's Kingdom-perspective.

Stay where you are. Hold on to your faith during the hard times, and depend on His goodness to lead and sustain you.

Expect to be blessed. Realize that the ultimate blessing comes from believing that God will do what He said He will do.

Dedicate everything to Christ. Realize that nothing will ever be as fulfilling as living for the One who gave Himself for you!

Blessed is she [and he] who believes in God's goodness, in His greater love, in His greatest plan!

Afterword

❧

This legacy of my journey with God and what He has shown me about Himself and His amazing *better* plans for my life began in February 2003, when God led me to the pages of Jeremiah 1 during my daily quiet time. God challenged and charged me to "write the words," and He assured me that He would give me the "words to write." After many delays, the process of writing started in earnest in mid-October in Bar Harbor, Maine, and was completed in Richmond Hill, Ontario, at the L'Arche Daybreak community. The process of reviewing the last thirty-one years has been one of prayer, reflection, and great blessing for me. To recount the work of God in my family has been a labor of love and an exercise of deep gratitude. The list of blessings God has given us throughout the years has been remarkable, and these pages relate only a few.

When I began these pages, it was my desire to share how I have learned that the greatest blessing of all is believing that God keeps His promises. "Blessed is she who has believed that what the Lord has said to her will be accomplished!" The blessing is in the believing; the blessing *is* the believing!

I have often wondered why God has chosen me to bless so abundantly. What makes me so special? I have come to believe that each one of us is God's favorite! Each one of us is the one Jesus loves,[1] and God has designed a *better* plan for each one of us. He is just waiting for us to want it. I began this endeavor knowing that I have indeed been "blessed to believe" in my life. But now, as I look back on the events that have transpired while I was writing these words—the places God arranged for me to write, the people He brought into the experience,

even the weather and scenery He provided for inspiration and intro-
spection—I am overwhelmed once more with just how wonderfully,
inconceivably, and inexhaustibly *good* God is.

> How precious are your thoughts about me, O God.
> They cannot be numbered! I can't even count them; they
> outnumber the grains of sand![2]

I pray that these words will somehow deepen your trust, edify your
faith, and encourage your belief in the goodness of God.

The following three appendixes contain resources that may help you as you seek to discover God's dream for your life. Use them in your private study, in whatever way is meaningful to you, to help you draw near to the Lord through prayer, stillness, Bible study, and journaling.

APPENDIX A
Names of God

Listed below are only some of the many names that God has given us to help us understand who He is and what He wants to be and do for us. As you read God's Word, begin to note and reflect on how great and sufficient the name of God is!

OLD TESTAMENT

Yahweh-Elohim	*The Supreme Lord God*	GENESIS 1:1
El Elyon	*Most High (the Strongest Mighty One)*	GENESIS 14:18
El Roi	*The Mighty One Who Sees*	GENESIS 16:13
El-Shaddai	*The Lord God Almighty*	GENESIS 17:1
El Olam	*Everlasting God*	GENESIS 21:33
Yahweh-Yireh	*The Lord Provides*	GENESIS 22:14
Yahweh/Jehovah	*I AM (the Self-Existent One)*	EXODUS 3:14-15
Yahweh-Rapha	*The Lord Who Heals*	EXODUS 15:26
Yahweh-Nissi	*The Lord Is My Banner (the Lord Who Goes before Me)*	EXODUS 17:15
Yahweh-Maccaddeshem	*The Lord Your Sanctifier*	EXODUS 31:3
Yahweh-Shalom	*The Lord of Peace*	JUDGES 6:24

Yahweh-Tsebaoth	The Lord of Hosts (the Lord over Multitudes of Heavenly Power)	1 SAMUEL 1:3
Yahweh-Raah	The Lord Is My Shepherd	PSALM 23:1
Elohim Adonai	The Lord Is My God	PSALM 86:12
Immanuel	God with Us	ISAIAH 7:14
Yahweh-Tsur	The Lord My Rock	ISAIAH 44:8
Yahweh-Ga'al	The Lord Redeemer	ISAIAH 48:17
Yahweh-Tsidkenu	The Lord Our Righteousness	JEREMIAH 23:6
Yahweh-El-Gemolah	The Lord God of Reward	JEREMIAH 51:56
Yahweh-Shammah	The Lord Is There	EZEKIEL 48:35

NEW TESTAMENT

Pater	Father	MATTHEW 5:16; 28:19
Numphios	Bridegroom	MARK 2:19
Abba	Papa	MARK 14:36
Theos Soter	The Supreme Deliverer	LUKE 1:47; 2:11
Poimen	Shepherd, Pastor	LUKE 15:4-7; JOHN 10:11-16
Logos	The Word	JOHN 1:1
Phos	The Light	JOHN 1:9
Christos	Christ, Messiah, the Anointed One	JOHN 1:41

JESUS SAID, "I AM . . ."

I am the Messiah	JOHN 4:26; 13:19
I am the Bread of Life	JOHN 6:35
I am the Light of the World	JOHN 8:12
I am the Gate	JOHN 10:7
I am the Good Shepherd	JOHN 10:11
I am the Son of God	JOHN 10:36
I am the Resurrection and the Life	JOHN 11:25
I am the Way, the Truth, and the Life	JOHN 14:6
I am the Vine	JOHN 15:1

Prayer and Solitude Guides

THE SOLITUDE EXPERIENCE

We live in noisy, busy times, and though our souls long to wait on God, it is often difficult to set aside time just to be still. Solitude is not about doing something; it is about being in the quiet presence of God. It is not about producing something; it is about becoming intimate with God.

In order to make the most of this time:

1. Set aside a period of time for God alone.
2. Select a quiet, comfortable place.
3. Eliminate as many distractions as possible.

- Have your Bible and pen with you.
- Use the spaces provided in this guide to record your insights and prayers.
- Turn off your cell phone.
- Some people find that quiet background music helps them focus on God and eliminate the intruding noises of our culture. However, do not let the music interfere with your focus on God's voice or intrude on the quiet of others.

4. Relax and take your time!
5. Desire, expect, and welcome the presence of God.

As you read on, you will find three templates to guide you through focused times of prayer and solitude. One centers on drawing closer to God, one closely examines Psalm 139, and the third highlights some of the key points and Scripture passages from this book. I pray that these will bless you on the journey to discovering God's dream for your life.

PRAYER AND SOLITUDE GUIDE 1: DRAW CLOSE TO GOD

The closer we are to God, the more we will be able to trust His plans for us. We draw close to God through seeing Him as He is, loving Him, listening to Him, embracing Him, and remaining in Him.

RECOGNIZE GOD

> This is the way to have eternal life—to know you, the only true God, and Jesus Christ, the one you sent to earth. JOHN 17:3

The names of God in the Bible reflect His character and ways. As you begin your quiet time, focus on the person of God and recognize who and what He is. God revealed Himself to Moses as "I AM WHO I AM."[1] The more you experience God and the more areas of your life you give to Him, the more intimately He will reveal Himself to you.

Using the following psalm, spend some time reflecting on who God is. Record any insights you receive in the space at the end of this section.

Psalm 145

> *I will exalt you, my God and King,*
> *and praise your name forever and ever.*

I will praise you every day;
yes, I will praise you forever.

Great is the LORD! He is most worthy of praise!
No one can measure his greatness.

Let each generation tell its children of your mighty acts;
let them proclaim your power.

I will meditate on your majestic, glorious splendor
and your wonderful miracles.

Your awe-inspiring deeds will be on every tongue;
I will proclaim your greatness.

Everyone will share the story of your wonderful goodness;
they will sing with joy about your righteousness.

The LORD is merciful and compassionate,
slow to get angry and filled with unfailing love.

The LORD is good to everyone.
He showers compassion on all his creation.

All of your works will thank you, LORD,
and your faithful followers will praise you.

They will speak of the glory of your kingdom;
they will give examples of your power.

They will tell about your mighty deeds
and about the majesty and glory of your reign.

For your kingdom is an everlasting kingdom.
You rule throughout all generations.

The LORD always keeps his promises;
he is gracious in all he does.

The LORD helps the fallen
and lifts those bent beneath their loads.

The eyes of all look to you in hope;
you give them their food as they need it.

When you open your hand,
you satisfy the hunger and thirst of every living thing.

The LORD is righteous in everything he does;
he is filled with kindness.

The LORD is close to all who call on him,
  yes, to all who call on him in truth.

He grants the desires of those who fear him;
  he hears their cries for help and rescues them.

The LORD protects all those who love him,
  but he destroys the wicked.

I will praise the LORD,
  and may everyone on earth bless his holy name
  forever and ever.

LOVE GOD

Jesus replied, "'You must love the LORD your God with
all your heart, all your soul, and all your mind.' This is
the first and greatest commandment. A second is equally
important: 'Love your neighbor as yourself.'" MATTHEW 22:37-39

God wants to share an intimate and loving relationship with you!
He wants you to know and worship Him and to love Him as much as
you can. We need to examine what things, attitudes, or behaviors
may be hindering or obstructing our love relationship with God.
Prayerfully consider the following passages and record any insights or
decisions you come to.

Fear the LORD and serve him wholeheartedly. Put away
forever the idols your ancestors worshiped when they
lived beyond the Euphrates River and in Egypt. Serve
the LORD alone. But if you refuse to serve the LORD,
then choose today whom you will serve. Would you pre-
fer the gods your ancestors served beyond the Euphrates? Or will it be the gods of the Amorites in whose land
you now live? But as for me and my family, we will serve
the LORD. JOSHUA 24:14-15

No one can serve two masters. For you will hate one and
love the other; you will be devoted to one and despise
the other. You cannot serve both God and money.

MATTHEW 6:24

Those who accept my commandments and obey them
are the ones who love me. And because they love me,
my Father will love them. And I will love them and
reveal myself to each of them.   JOHN 14:21

Just as you accepted Christ Jesus as your Lord, you must
continue to follow him. Let your roots grow down into
him, and let your lives be built on him. Then your faith
will grow strong in the truth you were taught, and you
will overflow with thankfulness.   COLOSSIANS 2:6-7

We can be sure that we know him if we obey his commandments. If someone claims, "I know God," but
doesn't obey God's commandments, that person is a liar
and is not living in the truth. But those who obey God's
word truly show how completely they love him. That is
how we know we are living in him.   1 JOHN 2:3-5

_____

_____

_____

_____

_____

_____

_____

_____

_____

LISTEN FOR GOD

He who belongs to God hears what God says. The
reason you do not hear is that you do not belong to
God. JOHN 8:47 (NIV)

Every true relationship is based on some kind of mutual communication. God desires communion with us, and that necessitates
two-way interaction. Too often our prayer lives are centered on our
talking to God rather than listening to what He is trying to tell us.
God uses the Holy Spirit to speak to us in many ways: through the
Bible, prayer, His creation, our circumstances, and other believers.
When God speaks to us, it is so we can know Him better and recognize His presence, His will, and His ways in our lives.

Take a few moments to sit and notice your environment. Reflect on
the evidences of God around you in what you see, hear, or sense.
Commit these evidences to your memory, contemplate on them, and
try to fully embrace the sensory experience (smell, sound, sight,
touch, and taste) of realizing God's presence.

Prayerfully consider and reflect on the following scriptural
responses to God's calling:

During the night God spoke to him in a vision. "Jacob!
Jacob!" he called. "Here I am," Jacob replied. GENESIS 46:2

When the LORD saw Moses coming to take a closer look,
God called to him from the middle of the bush, "Moses!
Moses!" "Here I am!" Moses replied. EXODUS 3:4

The LORD came and called as before, "Samuel! Samuel!"
And Samuel replied, "Speak, your servant is listening."

1 SAMUEL 3:10

Quietly, in your heart, respond to God's call to you.

_____

_____

_____

_____

_____

_____

_____

_____

EMBRACE GOD'S LOVE

Listen to the LORD who created you. O Israel, the one
who formed you says, "Do not be afraid, for I have ransomed you. I have called you by name; you are mine.
When you go through deep waters, I will be with you.
When you go through rivers of difficulty, you will not
drown. When you walk through the fire of oppression,
you will not be burned up; the flames will not consume
you. For I am the LORD, your God, the Holy One of
Israel, your Savior. ISAIAH 43:1-3

I would not forget you! See, I have written your name on
the palms of my hands. ISAIAH 49:15-16

Prayerfully reflect on the previous passages. Listen with your heart, and try to hear God's reassurance of His unending and unconditional devotion for you.

Consider the loving and gentle emotion behind these words. Try to feel God's immense and immeasurable love for you in these passages.

_____

_____

_____

_____

_____

_____

_____

REMAIN WITH GOD

And be sure of this: I am with you always. MATTHEW 28:20

Take a few moments to thank God for meeting you.

Remain in silence for a few more moments, contemplating what this time has meant to you. What have you felt, heard, or experienced in this quiet time and place?

Thank God for meeting you today and for loving you always.

Amen.

_____

_____

_____

_____

_____

_____

_____

_____

_____

PRAYER AND SOLITUDE GUIDE 2: PSALM 139

By showing us how intimately God sees and knows us, Psalm 139 gives us a beautiful picture of some significant attributes of God. Prayerfully read and reflect on the following psalm:

> O LORD, you have examined my heart
>   and know everything about me.
> You know when I sit down or stand up.
>   You know my thoughts even when I'm far away.
> You see me when I travel
>   and when I rest at home.
> You know everything I do.
> You know what I am going to say
>   even before I say it, LORD.
> You go before me and follow me.
>   You place your hand of blessing on my head.
> Such knowledge is too wonderful for me,
>   too great for me to understand!
> I can never escape from your Spirit!
>   I can never get away from your presence!
> If I go up to heaven, you are there;
>   if I go down to the grave, you are there.
> If I ride the wings of the morning,
>   if I dwell by the farthest oceans,

even there your hand will guide me,
and your strength will support me.

I could ask the darkness to hide me
and the light around me to become night—
but even in darkness I cannot hide from you.

To you the night shines as bright as day.
Darkness and light are the same to you.

You made all the delicate, inner parts of my body
and knit me together in my mother's womb.

Thank you for making me so wonderfully complex!
Your workmanship is marvelous—how well I know it.

You watched me as I was being formed in utter seclusion,
as I was woven together in the dark of the womb.

You saw me before I was born.
Every day of my life was recorded in your book.

Every moment was laid out
before a single day had passed.

How precious are your thoughts about me, O God.
They cannot be numbered!

I can't even count them;
they outnumber the grains of sand!

And when I wake up,
you are still with me!

O God, if only you would destroy the wicked!
Get out of my life, you murderers!

They blaspheme you;
your enemies misuse your name.

O LORD, shouldn't I hate those who hate you?
Shouldn't I despise those who oppose you?

Yes, I hate them with total hatred,
for your enemies are my enemies.

Search me, O God, and know my heart;
test me and know my anxious thoughts.

Point out anything in me that offends you,
and lead me along the path of everlasting life.

OMNISCIENT
You know me completely.

> O LORD, you have examined my heart and know every-
> thing about me. You know when I sit down or stand up.
> You know my thoughts even when I'm far away. You see
> me when I travel and when I rest at home. You know
> everything I do. You know what I am going to say even
> before I say it, LORD. (vv. 1-4)

Spend a few minutes thanking God that He is all-knowing and all-loving, that He knows everything about you, and that His love is unending! Record your thanksgiving.

_____

_____

_____

_____

_____

_____

_____

_____

_____

OMNIPRESENT
You are always with me.

> You go before me and follow me. You place your hand
> of blessing on my head. Such knowledge is too wonder-
> ful for me, too great for me to understand! (vv. 5-6)

You will never let me go.

> I can never escape from your Spirit! I can never get away
> from your presence! If I go up to heaven, you are there; if
> I go down to the grave, you are there. If I ride the wings
> of the morning, if I dwell by the farthest oceans, even
> there your hand will guide me, and your strength will
> support me. (vv. 7-10)

You will always be with me.

> I could ask the darkness to hide me and the light around
> me to become night—but even in darkness I cannot hide
> from you. To you the night shines as bright as day.
> Darkness and light are the same to you. (vv. 11-12)

Nothing can separate us from the love of our Father in heaven.
Before the creation of the world, God planned a way for us to be with
Him always. Paul tells us:

> Can anything ever separate us from Christ's love?
> Does it mean he no longer loves us if we have trouble or
> calamity, or are persecuted, or hungry, or destitute, or in
> danger, or threatened with death? (As the Scriptures say,
> "For your sake we are killed every day; we are being
> slaughtered like sheep.") No, despite all these things,
> overwhelming victory is ours through Christ, who loved
> us. And I am convinced that nothing can ever separate us
> from God's love. Neither death nor life, neither angels
> nor demons, neither our fears for today nor our worries
> about tomorrow—not even the powers of hell can sepa-
> rate us from God's love. No power in the sky above or in
> the earth below—indeed, nothing in all creation will

ever be able to separate us from the love of God that is
revealed in Christ Jesus our Lord. ROMANS 8:35-39

Spend some time reflecting on God's faithful presence in your life:
your past, your present, and your future. Record your response to
God's faithfulness.

_____

_____

_____

_____

_____

_____

_____

_____

_____

CREATOR

You created me; You planned me.

> You made all the delicate, inner parts of my body and
> knit me together in my mother's womb. Thank you for
> making me so wonderfully complex! Your workmanship
> is marvelous—how well I know it. You watched me as I
> was being formed in utter seclusion, as I was woven
> together in the dark of the womb. You saw me before I
> was born. Every day of my life was recorded in your
> book. Every moment was laid out before a single day had

passed. How precious are your thoughts about me,
O God. They cannot be numbered! I can't even count
them; they outnumber the grains of sand! And when I
wake up, you are still with me! (vv. 13-18)

Our Father in heaven has created us all intentionally and individually, according to His plan. Reflect on this amazing fact. Thankfully consider the many gifts, talents, and abilities He has programmed into you. Dedicate yourself and all He has given you to His full service!

HOLY

You are the standard I align myself to.

O God, if only you would destroy the wicked! Get out
of my life, you murderers! They blaspheme you; your
enemies misuse your name. O LORD, shouldn't I hate
those who hate you? Shouldn't I despise those who
oppose you? Yes, I hate them with total hatred, for your
enemies are my enemies. (vv. 19-22)

If we are going to be all God created us to be, it is important that we align ourselves with God's will and His ways. Through prayer and the knowledge of His Word, we are to be lights to this world and examples of His standard. Consider the following verses as you yield your principles, ideals, and motives to Him.

Let those who love the LORD hate evil, for he guards the
lives of his faithful ones and delivers them from the hand
of the wicked. Light is shed upon the righteous and joy
on the upright in heart. Rejoice in the LORD, you who
are righteous, and praise his holy name. PSALM 97:10-12 (NIV)

I gain understanding from your precepts; therefore I hate every wrong path. Your word is a lamp to my feet and a light for my path. PSALM 119:104-105 (NIV)

Pledge your alliance with God's standard and confess any struggles you have in this area.

_____

_____

_____

_____

_____

_____

_____

_____

GOOD

Make me usable.

Search me, O God, and know my heart; test me and know my anxious thoughts. Point out anything in me that offends you, and lead me along the path of everlasting life. (vv. 23-24)

Ask God to examine your heart, thoughts, motives, and desires. Ask Him to reveal any insincerity, fear, or unconfessed sin that would hinder your dedication and service to Him. Use the following verses to help you reflect.

I have considered my ways and have turned my steps to
your statutes. I will hasten and not delay to obey your
commands. PSALM 119:59-60 (NIV)

Let us examine our ways and test them, and let us return
to the LORD. LAMENTATIONS 3:40 (NIV)

Examine yourselves to see whether you are in the faith;
test yourselves. Do you not realize that Christ Jesus is in
you—unless, of course, you fail the test?
                                        2 CORINTHIANS 13:5 (NIV)

If anyone thinks he is something when he is nothing, he
deceives himself. Each one should test his own actions.
Then he can take pride in himself, without comparing
himself to somebody else, for each one should carry his
own load. GALATIANS 6:3-5 (NIV)

Close by reflecting on the following verse:

Praise be to the God and Father of our Lord Jesus Christ,
who has blessed us in the heavenly realms with every
spiritual blessing in Christ. For he chose us in him before
the creation of the world to be holy and blameless in his
sight. In love he predestined us to be adopted as his sons
through Jesus Christ, in accordance with his pleasure and
will—to the praise of his glorious grace, which he has
freely given us in the One he loves. EPHESIANS 1:3-6 (NIV)
Amen.

PRAYER AND SOLITUDE GUIDE 3:
B.L.E.S.S.E.D. TO BELIEVE

> You are blessed because you believed that the Lord
> would do what he said. LUKE 1:45

Scripture tells us that Mary, the mother of Jesus, was blessed because she believed that God would do what He said He would do. Her confidence in God was so certain that she responded to His messenger, "I am the Lord's servant. May everything you have said about me come true."[2]

Mary was willing for God to interrupt her plans for His *better* plans! God has better plans for our lives than we could ever imagine for ourselves. But how do we become available for God's intervention? How can we begin to live *B.L.E.S.S.E.D.* lives? The chapters throughout this book form an acronym that tells us how:

Believe in God's goodness

Let go of your agenda

Embrace reality

See from God's heart

Stay where you are

Expect to be blessed

Dedicate everything to Christ

BELIEVE IN GOD'S GOODNESS

> The LORD is just! He is my rock! There is no evil in him!
> PSALM 92:15

If we desire to live truly blessed, we must choose to believe in the unchanging goodness of God and the unquestionable goodness of everything He does and provides. He is the Good Shepherd, the source of every good and worthy thing, and the constructor and completer of His good works.

Prayerfully reflect on the following thoughts and Scripture passages.

THE GOODNESS OF WHO GOD IS

Goodness is an attribute of God; it is part of His very nature and the quality of who He is.

> Taste and see that the LORD is good. Oh, the joys of those who take refuge in him! PSALM 34:8

> The LORD is good. His unfailing love continues forever, and his faithfulness continues to each generation. PSALM 100:5

THE GOODNESS OF WHAT GOD GIVES

It is God's nature to give. All that He gives flows from His goodness. Regardless of our circumstances, and whether or not it seems that God is listening or answering our prayers, God is giving His children good things. The apostle Matthew records Jesus' teaching:

> You parents—if your children ask for a loaf of bread, do you give them a stone instead? Or if they ask for a fish, do you give them a snake? Of course not! So if you sinful people know how to give good gifts to your children, how much more will your heavenly Father give good gifts to those who ask him. MATTHEW 7:9-11

The Goodness of What God Does

God is the definition of goodness. From His creation to His plan of redemption to the eventual total reconciliation of His creation to Himself, everything God does demonstrates His goodness.

God looked over all he had made, and he saw that it was
very good! GENESIS 1:31

God showed his great love for us by sending Christ to
die for us while we were still sinners. And since we have
been made right in God's sight by the blood of Christ,
he will certainly save us from God's condemnation. For
since our friendship with God was restored by the death
of his Son while we were still his enemies, we will certainly be saved through the life of his Son. So now we
can rejoice in our wonderful new relationship with God
because our Lord Jesus Christ has made us friends of
God. ROMANS 5:8-11

Reflections:

_____

_____

_____

_____

_____

_____

_____

_____

_____

LET GO OF MY AGENDA

> I will open the windows of heaven for you. I will pour
> out a blessing so great you won't have enough room to
> take it in! MALACHI 3:10

God has a better design for our lives than any we can devise for ourselves. His agenda for His children is a blessed life, a righteous life, a life lived for great purposes and by great principles. To accept God's agenda, we must first be willing to set our own plans aside and then wait for His plan to unfold in our lives.

Prayerfully reflect on the following thoughts and Scripture passages.

ACCEPT GOD'S TRUTH

What we believe affects every part of our lives. To open the pathway to God's plan for us, we need to decide, once and for all, if we are going to believe that God's Word is true for every situation.

> All your words are true; all your righteous laws are
> eternal. PSALM 119:160 (NIV)

ACCEPT MY POWERLESSNESS

One of the primary obstacles we have in letting go and letting God control our lives is our illusion that we somehow have the power to accomplish significant things. Jesus taught that on our own we can't even change one hair on our heads from black to white or add one extra day to our lives.[3] In fact, Jesus said that anything we accomplish that is not rooted in Him will ultimately amount to nothing.

> I am the vine; you are the branches. Those who remain
> in me, and I in them, will produce much fruit. For apart
> from me you can do nothing. JOHN 15:5

ACCEPT NEW POSSIBILITIES

God's design often seems beyond our comprehension. He does things differently than we would; He sees potential where we see problems. A crucial step to our accepting new possibilities is to abandon the need to understand.

> "My thoughts are nothing like your thoughts," says the Lord. "And my ways are far beyond anything you could imagine. For just as the heavens are higher than the earth, so my ways are higher than your ways and my thoughts higher than your thoughts." ISAIAH 55:8-9

Reflections:

_____

_____

_____

_____

_____

_____

_____

EMBRACE REALITY

> No eye has seen, no ear has heard, and no mind has imagined what God has prepared for those who love him. 1 CORINTHIANS 2:9

It is *today* that God wants to bless, and it is *now* that God wants to use. But He will use only the truth of today, not our illusions. If we

want to be in a place of blessing, if we want to experience the fullness
that God has for us, we need to be fully present for Him *today*!

Prayerfully reflect on the following thoughts and Scripture
passages.

RELEASE THE PAST

We must allow God to release us from our painful memories so that
He will be able to move us onward for His purposes. God will, and
can, use our past to bless our lives and the lives of others through us—
today—if we allow Him to. God told Israel:

> Forget the former things; do not dwell on the past. See, I
> am doing a new thing! Now it springs up; do you not
> perceive it? ISAIAH 43:18-19 (NIV)

REALIZE THE PRESENT

We are here by God's planning, and God has a purpose for us in just
this place! Our greatest significance can be realized only when we
comprehend how important it is to base our lives on something more
substantial than feelings and more reliable than chance.

> Who knows if perhaps you [are here] for just such a time
> as this? ESTHER 4:14

RELINQUISH TODAY

The greatest barrier to releasing our dreams and actions to God is
fear. Yet the greatest power we will ever experience is the power of
letting go and allowing God to become more and more the center of
our choices, decisions, and priorities.

> "Don't be afraid," he said, "for you are very precious to
> God. Peace! Be encouraged! Be strong!" DANIEL 10:19

Reflections:

_____

_____

_____

_____

_____

_____

_____

_____

_____

_____

SEE FROM GOD'S HEART

You are blessed because you believed that the Lord
would do what he said. LUKE 1:45

We judge goodness and worth by subjective standards of good—
measurements based largely on our personal perceptions of value. We
need to retrain ourselves to evaluate our world and our lives from a
different standard. We need to develop the ability to see God, ourselves, and others from the perspective of God's heart.

Prayerfully reflect on the following thoughts and Scripture
passages.

SEEING GOD: LOVING FATHER

God is God Almighty, the Creator of all things, the sovereign ruler
and authority over everything! But He is also Abba, Papa—merciful,

gentle, and good Father—who has gone to all lengths to have an intimate relationship of trust, love, and total security with His beloved
children.

> For God loved the world so much that he gave his one
> and only Son, so that everyone who believes in him will
> not perish but have eternal life. God sent his Son into
> the world not to judge the world, but to save the world
> through him. JOHN 3:16-17

SEEING SELF: BELOVED CHILD OF GOD

When I acknowledge that God has created me for the privilege of
glorifying Him and being loved by Him—that Abba, Papa God, cares
about my every need, promises never to leave me, and always keeps
His promises—I begin to loosen my self-centeredness. I allow myself
to start feeling loved as an adored child of God.

> While he was still a long way off, his father saw him
> coming. Filled with love and compassion, he ran to his
> son, embraced him, and kissed him. LUKE 15:20-21

> See how very much our Father loves us, for he calls us
> his children, and that is what we are! 1 JOHN 3:1

SEEING OTHERS: BELOVED FAMILY MEMBERS

Seeing others from God's heart is to see them for who they are—precious, adored children of God, no matter what their condition or circumstance. To love others as ourselves is to realize that we are all a
part of God's plan and therefore a part of each other. We share God's
vision for each other, and we share God's intention for each other—
to be loved and to love.

Everyone who believes that Jesus is the Christ has become a child of God. And everyone who loves the Father loves his children, too.   1 JOHN 5:1

Anyone who welcomes a little child . . . on my behalf welcomes me, and anyone who welcomes me also welcomes my Father who sent me. Whoever is the least among you is the greatest.   LUKE 9:48

Reflections:

_____

_____

_____

_____

_____

_____

_____

_____

_____

_____

STAY WHERE YOU ARE

Despite all these things, overwhelming victory is ours through Christ, who loved us.   ROMANS 8:37

The gift of joy that is found in suffering is the opportunity to completely rely only on God long enough to experience His power, His provision, and His presence in character-changing ways. Experiential knowledge of God's faithfulness produces the hope that will not disappoint—hope based on the love that God pours out on us as we depend upon Him.

There comes a time when all we can do is hold on and believe what God has told us. It is a time of *staying*.

Prayerfully reflect on the following thoughts and Scripture passages.

> Can anything ever separate us from Christ's love? Does it mean he no longer loves us if we have trouble or calamity, or are persecuted, or hungry, or destitute, or in danger, or threatened with death? . . . No, despite all these things, overwhelming victory is ours through Christ, who loved us. ROMANS 8:35-37

STAYING OBEDIENT
Regardless of the circumstances around us, we continue to do the things we need to do.

> Let's not get tired of doing what is good. At just the right time we will reap a harvest of blessing if we don't give up. GALATIANS 6:9

STAYING FAITHFUL
Regardless of our feelings, we choose to believe that all things are possible and that even if we never see the fulfillment of God's promises in this life, He will do what He says He will do!

> Humanly speaking, it is impossible. But not with God. Everything is possible with God. MARK 10:27

STAYING WHERE WE ARE
Even when we want to withdraw, we depend for a season on the body of believers we are a part of, allowing them to give us support and encouragement.

> We are many parts of one body, and we all belong to each other. ROMANS 12:5

STAYING IN AN ATTITUDE OF LOVE
Even when we hate the situation we find ourselves in, we intentionally resolve to remain in love.

> Love never gives up, never loses faith, is always hopeful, and endures through every circumstance. 1 CORINTHIANS 13:7

Reflections:

_____

_____

_____

_____

_____

_____

_____

_____

_____

EXPECT TO BE BLESSED

"For I know the plans I have for you," says the LORD.
"They are plans for good and not for disaster, to give
you a future and a hope. In those days when you pray, I
will listen. If you look for me wholeheartedly, you will
find me. I will be found by you," says the LORD. "I will
end your captivity and restore your fortunes. I will
gather you out of the nations where I sent you and will
bring you home again to your own land." JEREMIAH 29:11-14

God is in the business of changing things—changing pain into triumph, dreams into realities, and lives into blessings. But if we do not
expect the blessing, we just might miss it! Being blessed by the sovereign Creator of the universe is an overwhelmingly awesome experience, and expecting to be blessed by the sovereign Creator of the
universe is a humble expectation.

Prayerfully reflect on the following thoughts and Scripture
passages.

LOOKING FORWARD TO BLESSING: ENTITLEMENT
VERSUS EXPECTATION

God blesses us because it is His pleasure to do so, not because we in
any way warrant it. That is called grace—God's unmerited, undeserved, and unearned favor.

My Father is always working, and so am I. JOHN 5:17

LOOKING FOR BLESSING: LIVING THE LIFE GOD BLESSES

God works where His will is being done! God works where His name
is being called on. God works where His people are actively serving
and working in His name. To find God's "blessing ground," we must
be living in accordance with what God blesses.

You can ask for anything in my name, and I will do it, so
that the Son can bring glory to the Father.   JOHN 14:13

RECEIVING BLESSING: AWE AND WONDER

To receive God's unexpected blessings, we must be available for Him
to bless—living in His blessing ground and looking for His presence
and power in our midst. Then we must be ready and willing to receive
what He is holding out to us, whether or not it makes sense at the
moment. We accept it with complete trust that if it's from God it is
therefore good and if it's good, God will fulfill His promises and purposes through it.

I am the Lord's servant. May everything you have said
about me come true. LUKE 1:38

Reflections:

_____

_____

_____

_____

_____

_____

_____

_____

_____

DEDICATE EVERYTHING TO CHRIST

Whatever you do, whether in word or deed, do it all in
the name of the Lord Jesus, giving thanks to God the
Father through him. COLOSSIANS 3:17 (NIV)

The blessing always begins with believing, but the blessing multiplies when we dedicate it back to Christ for His glory, His use, and
His purposes. The greatest blessing of all is having the Lord of the
universe walk through our troubles with us. Immanuel—God with us!
God has promised us:

> Do not be afraid, for I have ransomed you. I have called
> you by name; you are mine. When you go through deep
> waters, I will be with you. When you go through rivers
> of difficulty, you will not drown. When you walk
> through the fire of oppression, you will not be burned
> up; the flames will not consume you. For I am the LORD,
> your God, the Holy One of Israel, your Savior. ISAIAH 43:1-3

The path of blessing is not an easy path; it is not a comfortable
path; it is not a particularly prestigious or pretty path. But it is a *better*
path, a *blessed* path, and a *beautiful* path—it's the path traveled with the
Lord God Himself!

LOVE COMPLETELY

The love we give to and receive from God weaves our lives into a
beautiful cycle of faith. The more we love God, the more we will
depend on Him and trust Him to use our lives for His plan and purposes. As we experience the complete sufficiency and abundance of
His love, we will love Him even more! Jesus told us:

> The most important commandment is this: "Listen,
> O Israel! The Lord our God is the one and only Lord.

And you must love the Lord your God with all your
heart, all your soul, all your mind, and all your strength."

MARK 12:29-30

SERVE UNPRETENTIOUSLY

The path of servanthood is the intentional practice of putting others'
needs above our own because we have confidence that our Father is
taking care of us. It means giving to others because we realize that our
precious Lord gave everything for us. Jesus said:

I am giving you a new commandment: Love each other.
Just as I have loved you, you should love each other.
Your love for one another will prove to the world that
you are my disciples. JOHN 13:34-35

Reflections:

_____

_____

_____

_____

_____

_____

_____

_____

_____

You are blessed because you believed that the Lord
would do what he said. LUKE 1:45

Believe in God's goodness, regardless of your circumstances.

Let go of your agenda. Allow God to plan a better life for you.

Embrace reality. Accept the truth of your life, and let God use it for His glory.

See from God's heart. Train yourself to see from a Kingdom perspective.

Stay where you are. Hold on to your faith, and depend on God's providence.

Expect to be blessed. Look for and receive God's fulfillment.

Dedicate everything to Christ. Live for the One who died for you!

Fear Not

❧

Below is a partial list of the many "fear not" statements God has given us in Scripture. Fear short-circuits God's plans for us. He has provided His assurances so that we will be willing to live out His plans. You may want to make a note of all the "fear not" and "don't be afraid" statements you find as you read through the Bible. There is at least one for every day of the year!

- "The LORD spoke to Abram in a vision and said to him, 'Do not be afraid, Abram, for I will protect you, and your reward will be great.'" (Genesis 15:1)

- "Do not be afraid, for I am with you and will bless you." (Genesis 26:24)

- "'I am God, the God of your father,' the voice said. 'Do not be afraid to go down to Egypt, for there I will make your family into a great nation. I will go with you down to Egypt, and I will bring you back again.'" (Genesis 46:3-4)

- "Do not be afraid of him, for I have given you victory." (Deuteronomy 3:2)

- "Don't be afraid of them! Just remember what the LORD your God did to Pharaoh and to all the land of Egypt. Remember the great terrors the LORD your God sent against them. You saw it all with your own eyes! And remember the miraculous signs and wonders, and the strong hand and powerful arm with which he brought you out of Egypt. The LORD your God will use this same power against all the people you fear." (Deuteronomy 7:18-19)

- "This is my command—be strong and courageous! Do not be afraid or discouraged. For the LORD your God is with you wherever you go." (Joshua 1:9)

- "Do not be afraid or discouraged. Take all your fighting men and attack Ai, for I have given you the king of Ai, his people, his town, and his land." (Joshua 8:1)

- "'Do not be afraid of them,' the LORD said to Joshua, 'for I have given you victory over them. Not a single one of them will be able to stand up to you.'" (Joshua 10:8)

- "Elijah said to her, 'Don't be afraid! Go ahead and do just what you've said, but make a little bread for me first. Then use what's left to prepare a meal for yourself and your son. For this is what the LORD, the God of Israel, says: There will always be flour and olive oil left in your containers until the time when the LORD sends rain and the crops grow again!'" (1 Kings 17:13-14)

- "'Don't be afraid!' Elisha told him. 'For there are more on our side than on theirs!' Then Elisha prayed, 'O LORD, open his eyes and let him see!' The LORD opened the young man's eyes, and when he looked up, he saw that the hillside around Elisha was filled with horses and chariots of fire." (2 Kings 6:16-17)

- "Don't be afraid or discouraged, for the LORD God, my God, is with you. He will not fail you or forsake you." (1 Chronicles 28:20)

- "Don't be afraid of the enemy! Remember the Lord, who is great and glorious, and fight for your brothers, your sons, your daughters, your wives, and your homes!" (Nehemiah 4:14)

- "I will not be afraid, for you are close beside me." (Psalm 23:4)

- "The LORD is for me, so I will have no fear. What can mere people do to me?" (Psalm 118:6)

- "Don't be afraid, for I am with you. Don't be discouraged, for I am your God. I will strengthen you and help you. I will hold you up with my victorious right hand." (Isaiah 41:10)

- "Do not be afraid, for I have ransomed you. I have called you by name; you are mine. When you go through deep waters, I will be with you. When you go through rivers of difficulty, you will not drown. When you walk through the fire of oppression, you will not be burned up; the flames will not consume you. For I am the LORD, your God, the Holy One of Israel, your Savior. . . . You are precious to me. You are honored, and I love you." (Isaiah 43:1-4)

- "Do not be afraid, for I am with you. I will gather you and your children from east and west." (Isaiah 43:5-6)

- "Do not tremble; do not be afraid. Did I not proclaim my purposes for you long ago?" (Isaiah 44:8)

- "Don't be afraid of the people, for I will be with you and will protect you. I, the LORD, have spoken!" (Jeremiah 1:8)

- "I will appoint responsible shepherds who will care for them, and they will never be afraid again. Not a single one will be lost or missing." (Jeremiah 23:4)

- "'Do not be afraid, Jacob, my servant; do not be dismayed, Israel,' says the LORD. 'For I will bring you home again from distant lands, and your children will return from their exile. Israel will return to a life of peace and quiet, and no one will terrorize them. For I am with you and will save you,' says the LORD." (Jeremiah 30:10-11)

- "'Do not fear the king of Babylon anymore,' says the LORD. 'For I am with you and will save you and rescue you from his power.'" (Jeremiah 42:11)

- "Do not be afraid, Jacob, my servant; do not be dismayed, Israel. For I will bring you home again from distant lands, and your children will return from their exile." (Jeremiah 46:27)

- "'Do not be afraid, Jacob, my servant, for I am with you,' says the LORD. 'I will completely destroy the nations to which I have exiled you, but I will not completely destroy you. I will discipline you, but with justice; I cannot let you go unpunished.'" (Jeremiah 46:28)

- "'Don't be afraid,' he said, 'for you are very precious to God. Peace! Be encouraged! Be strong!'" (Daniel 10:19)

- "Cheer up, Zion! Don't be afraid! For the LORD your God is living among you. He is a mighty savior. He will take delight in you with gladness. With his love, he will calm all your fears. He will rejoice over you with joyful songs." (Zephaniah 3:16-17)

- "I will rescue you and make you both a symbol and a source of blessing. So don't be afraid." (Zechariah 8:13)

- "Jesus spoke to them at once. 'Don't be afraid,' he said. 'Take courage. I am here!'" (Matthew 14:27)

- "Don't be afraid. . . . God has heard your prayer." (Luke 1:13)

- "Don't be afraid. Just have faith." (Luke 8:50)

- "Don't be afraid, little flock. For it gives your Father great happiness to give you the Kingdom." (Luke 12:32)

- "I am leaving you with a gift—peace of mind and heart. And the peace I give is a gift the world cannot give. So don't be troubled or afraid." (John 14:27)

- "Don't be afraid! Speak out! Don't be silent! For I am with you." (Acts 18:9-10)

- "Don't be afraid! I am the First and the Last. I am the living one. I died, but look—I am alive forever and ever!" (Revelation 1:17-18)

Author's Note

For more information about Henri Nouwen and L'Arche Daybreak, contact the Henri Nouwen Society, 10265 Yonge St., Richmond Hill, ON L4C 4Y7, Canada; or PO Box 230523, Ansonia Station, New York, NY 10023.

Epilogue

WHERE THEY ARE NOW

Recently, as the final work on this book was being completed, we celebrated Greg's birthday with a surprise family reunion here in California. Joshua was the first to arrive from Canada. He and his wife, Meghan, still live in the Toronto area and remain active in the L'Arche Daybreak community. Next to turn up was Nick. He and Polly live with their son, Gabriel, in Texas. Polly is an accomplished artist, and Nick continues to work in construction. From Colorado, Suzanne and husband, Andy, arrived, fresh from a recent camping trip in the Rockies.

Nori has recently relocated from Chicago back to California to complete her PhD while teaching at a private university. Michelle, an elementary school teacher, and her husband, Teddy, also celebrated their sixth wedding anniversary this weekend with their three-year-old daughter, Savannah. And Christopher acted as official chauffeur, shuttling the out-of-town arrivals from the airport to their destination in secret synchronization with Dad's activities.

Everyone worked together to schedule every detail down to the last minute so that just as Greg arrived home from his daily six-mile run, the whole family was there to yell "Surprise!" . . . and we almost pulled it off! Our family has lived an exciting journey. From the broken dreams of two young newlyweds, God has created a family that continues to grow—in size, love, and laughter!

BELIEVING YOU'RE B.L.E.S.S.E.D.

There is one final PS to this story. As this book was being prepared, we had a dramatic revelation concerning our son Joshua. As he read what I had written and we talked about the details of his life from his perspective, we became aware of a terrible lie that he had lived with for more than a decade. As a teenager, Joshua was told in rehab, in an effort to control his behavior, that we, his parents, had disowned him and had made him a ward of the state. For the next twelve years, Josh believed this lie to be the truth—the truth about his parents and the truth about himself. Over the years, though he had forgiven us and reconciled with us, he always believed that we had disowned him. And of course, because Greg and I were completely unaware of it, it was always an unspoken burden in Josh's life. We praise God that the truth was finally revealed, that the lie has been exposed, and that the truth has brought us closer than ever.

Even though it was lie, because Josh believed it to be true, it affected every part of his life: the way he lived, the way he saw himself, and the choices he made. Some of us live believing a lie about our heavenly Father. We believe that because of our past or our failures or our insecurities, we have been disowned by God, and this prevents us from accepting that we are in fact His beloved children. Are you believing a lie? Do you know that you are a beloved child of God, whom He will never disown? Do not live as a disowned child! Believe that God has a dream for you. Live B.L.E.S.S.E.D.!

ENDNOTES

INTRODUCTION

1 ACTS 4:12

2 SEE ROMANS 3:23.

3 ACTS 17:11 (NIV)

CHAPTER 1

1 MARK 10:18

2 DEUTERONOMY 8:3

3 EXODUS 16:28-29

4 PSALM 119:35, 105

5 ISAIAH 26:7

6 ISAIAH 43:2

7 JOHN 10:11-16

8 ISAIAH 44:2-4

9 MALACHI 3:10

10 JOHN 14:2; MATTHEW 22:2

11 MATTHEW 7:9-11

12 LUKE 12:27-32

13 JAMES 1:17-18

14 JOHN 1:12

15 ROMANS 5:5

16 1 CORINTHIANS 12:4

17 SEE ROMANS 6:23.

18 GENESIS 1:1-4, 27-31

19 ROMANS 5:8-11

20 MATTHEW 20:28

21 GALATIANS 5:22-23

22 PSALM 92:15

23 PSALM 34:8-10

24 NAHUM 1:7

25 HEBREWS 10:35

CHAPTER 2

1 ROMANS 8:28

2 2 TIMOTHY 3:16-17

3 2 PETER 1:20-21

4 PSALM 119:160

5 PSALM 22:4-5

6 HEBREWS 6:18-19

7 MATTHEW 5:36; 6:27

8 JOHN 15:5

9 1 CORINTHIANS 3:13-15

10 ISAIAH 14:26-27

11 ISAIAH 55:8-9

12 1 CORINTHIANS 1:27-29

13 MALACHI 3:10

14 SEE 1 SAMUEL 15:22;
PSALM 51:17; JEREMIAH
7:21-23.

15 BRUCE SPRINGSTEEN,
"NO SURRENDER," FROM
BORN IN THE U.S.A. (1984).

16 GENESIS 1:26-27

17 GALATIANS 6:10;
COLOSSIANS 4:5-6

18 SEE MATTHEW 25:37-46;
HEBREWS 13:2.

19 SEE LUKE 10:30-37.

20 ROMANS 12:6-8

21 1 CORINTHIANS 6:19

22 SEE ROMANS 8:9.

23 ROMANS 12:2

CHAPTER 3

1 JOEL 2:25

2 PROVERBS 22:6 (NIV)

3 JOHN 8:32, EMPHASIS
ADDED

4 GALATIANS 1:13;
ACTS 22:4

5 PHILIPPIANS 3:13-14

6 ISAIAH 43:18-19 (NIV)

7 2 CORINTHIANS 1:3-4

8 SEE ROMANS 8:28.

9 ISAIAH 43:1-4

10 ISAIAH 49:15-16

11 1 CORINTHIANS 2:9

12 ESTHER 4:14

13 PSALM 119:105

14 JOHN 14:21, 23,
EMPHASIS ADDED

15 GALATIANS 5:17-18

16 MATTHEW 5:17

17 SEE ROMANS 3:31.

18 ROMANS 6:16

19 JOSHUA 24:15

CHAPTER 4

1 JOHN 3:3, 5-7, 15-16

[2] PSALM 44:14

[3] MATTHEW 11:30

[4] PSALM 6:6-7

[5] PSALM 88:13-18

[6] LUKE 1:45 (NIV)

[7] LUKE 1:28-45, EMPHASIS ADDED

[8] GENESIS 1:31

[9] MARK 12:28-31

[10] MATTHEW 7:9-11

[11] SEE LUKE 11:13.

[12] 1 CORINTHIANS 2:10, 12

[13] LUKE 1:45 (NIV)

[14] PHILIPPIANS 4:7

[15] JOHN 13:23

[16] MARK 3:17; LUKE 9:52-56

[17] SEE LUKE 9:56 (NKJV).

[18] JOHN 8:1-11

[19] MATTHEW 11:28

[20] JOHN 17:21

[21] ECCLESIASTES 1:9

[22] GALATIANS 5:22-23

[23] PHILIPPIANS 4:8 (NIV)

[24] SEE MATTHEW 19:14.

CHAPTER 5

[1] GENESIS 32:26-30

[2] ROMANS 5:3-5 (NIV)

[3] MATTHEW 19:26; MARK 10:27

[4] 1 CORINTHIANS 13:7

[5] ROMANS 8:35-37

[6] ACTS 20:24

[7] PSALM 37:7; 46:10 (NIV)

[8] ISAIAH 30:18 (NIV)

[9] HEBREWS 4:12 (NIV)

[10] EXODUS 3:14

[11] EXODUS 15:2

[12] MATTHEW 1:23

[13] JOHN 1:9

[14] GENESIS 22:14

[15] HABAKKUK 2:1-3

[16] REVELATION 3:20 (NIV)

[17] SEE EPHESIANS 4:4-6.

[18] ACTS 2:46-47

[19] SEE ROMANS 16:5 AND 1 CORINTHIANS 16:19.

[20] SEE MARK 2:1-12 AND LUKE 5:17-26.

[21] PSALM 6:6

[22] GENESIS 2:20-24

[23] SEE 1 CORINTHIANS 12.

CHAPTER 6

[1] JEREMIAH 29:10-11, EMPHASIS ADDED

[2] 1 CORINTHIANS 12:3

[3] HENRI J. M. NOUWEN, LETTERS TO MARC ABOUT JESUS (SAN FRANCISCO: HARPER AND ROW, 1987).

[4] FOR MORE INFORMATION ABOUT HENRI NOUWEN AND L'ARCHE DAYBREAK

COMMUNITY, CONTACT L'ARCHE DAYBREAK, 11339 YONGE ST., RICHMOND HILL, ON L4S 1L1, CANADA.

[5] PHILIPPIANS 1:6 (NIV)

[6] PSALM 23:5

[7] SEE ROMANS 9:11-33.

[8] JOHN 5:17

[9] PHILIPPIANS 4:13 (NASB)

[10] SEE MATTHEW 4:19; 8:22; 9:9; 16:24; 19:21; MARK 2:14; LUKE 5:27; 9:59; JOHN 1:43; 12:26; 21:22.

[11] SEE MATTHEW 5:3-10.

[12] LUKE 1:38

[13] LUKE 1:46-49

[14] WILLIAM SHAKESPEARE, AS YOU LIKE IT (ACT 2, SCENE 7).

[15] ISAIAH 64:8-9

[16] SEE ROMANS 8:29; 2 CORINTHIANS 5:17; AND EPHESIANS 4:23.

[17] 2 CORINTHIANS 3:17-18 (NIV)

[18] SEE ROMANS 12:2.

[19] PHILIPPIANS 2:5

[20] JAMES 3:17-18

[21] JEREMIAH 29:11-14

CHAPTER 7

[1] MATTHEW 5:9 (NKJV)

[2] COLOSSIANS 3:17 (NIV)

³ NIV

⁴ MARK 14:36

⁵ PSALM 65:11

⁶ ISAIAH 43:1-3

⁷ MATTHEW 1:23 TELLS US
THAT JESUS IS IMMANUEL,
GOD IS WITH US.

⁸ MARK 12:29-30

⁹ 1 JOHN 4:16-18

¹⁰ JOHN 13:34-35

¹¹ JOHN 13:4-5, 12-17

¹² LUKE 12:22-34

¹³ GALATIANS 5:6

¹⁴ JAMES 1:27

¹⁵ ISAIAH 58:6-7

¹⁶ SEE MATTHEW 25:31-46.

¹⁷ ISAIAH 58:10-11

¹⁸ ISAIAH 53:3

¹⁹ MATTHEW 26:26; MARK
14:22; 1 CORINTHIANS
11:23-24

²⁰ REVELATION 17:14;
19:16

²¹ EPHESIANS 5:20 (NIV)

²² PHILIPPIANS 4:8

²³ ZECHARIAH 4:10

²⁴ PHILIPPIANS 4:4-7 (NIV)

²⁵ 1 PETER 1:15-16

²⁶ 1 THESSALONIANS
3:12-13

²⁷ 1 CORINTHIANS 1:2

²⁸ COLOSSIANS 3:16-17

²⁹ SEE PSALM 19 FOR A
BEAUTIFUL TRIBUTE TO
GOD'S GLORY SEEN
THROUGH HIS CREATION.

³⁰ REVELATION 5:11-14

³¹ 1 PETER 4:10-11

³² ACTS 1:8

³³ MATTHEW 28:19-20

³⁴ ACTS 4:12

³⁵ SEE MATTHEW 27–28;
MARK 15–16; LUKE 23–24;
JOHN 19–20; ACTS
13:23-31; AND
1 CORINTHIANS 15:3-8.

³⁶ GALATIANS 2:21

³⁷ 2 CORINTHIANS 5:17-21

CONCLUSION

¹ EPHESIANS 3:18-19

² ISAIAH 7:14; MATTHEW
1:23

³ GENESIS 15:5

⁴ GENESIS 15:6

⁵ MARK 14:32-36

⁶ MATTHEW 26:47, 52-54

⁷ EPHESIANS 1:4-5, 9,
EMPHASIS ADDED

⁸ EPHESIANS 1:11

⁹ EPHESIANS 1:3, 6-8,
13-14, EMPHASIS ADDED

¹⁰ EPHESIANS 1:10

AFTERWORD

¹ SEE JOHN 13:23; 19:26;
20:2; AND 21:7.

² PSALM 139:17-18

APPENDIX B

¹ EXODUS 3:13-14

² LUKE 1:38

³ MATTHEW 5:36; 6:27